SOUTHWICK

THE

D-DAY VILLAGE

THAT WENT TO WAR

by

Ashford, Buchan
& Enright
P O Box 20
Leatherhead
Surrey KT24 5HH

CONTENTS

ILLUSTRATIONS & PLANS

PHOTO ACKNOWLEDGEMENTS

By Courtesy of The News, Portsmouth
Pages 16, 18, 20, 38, 40, 42, 44, 46, 48, 50, 52, 54, 56, 58, 64, 66, 68, 70, 72, 76, 84, 86, 88, 90, 94, 98, 101, 105, 106, 107, 108, 114, 116, 120, 128, 130

By Courtesy of The Daily Express
Pages 78

By Courtesy of the Trustees of the Imperial War Museum, London
Pages 66, 68, 74, 76, 80, 82, 84, 86, 88, 90, 92, 98, 101, 102, 103, 104, 109, 110, 111, 112, 114, 116, 118, 120

By Courtesy of Picture Post
Pages 34, 36

By Courtesy of HMS Dryad
Pages 22, 126, 128, 132, 134, 136

By Courtesy of The D-Day Museum, Portsmouth
98, 109, 122, 126

Private Collection
Pages 8, 12, 14, 16, 97, 99, 100, 104

FOREWORD

It was not many years after my first professional efforts as an author that the 40th anniversary of D-Day loomed large. I had been engaged for a considerable period in the research necessary to author my *magnus opus* - Secretive Southwick Domesday to D-Day. That year I managed to both write and publish a guide to Crete, the Southwick history as well as a small booklet about Southwick's involvement in the Second World War. The latter was simply an extract of the last few chapters from the major work.

For the 50th celebrations I have chosen to write a totally new book detailing the village's fascinating and unique place in the last great global conflict. For it was at Southwick House that the Allied Supreme Commander, General Eisenhower, made the fateful decision to launch the invasion of Europe on D-Day. An invasion which liberated Europe and led to the final demise of Hitler's Third Reich. The Fuhrer's rule was planned to last a thousand years, not the decade or so that the Nazis managed to hold on to power by tyranny and fear. It is thought provoking that, at the time of the war, the family owning Southwick Mansion had held feudal sway, over the local area, for some 400 years. *En passant*, they continue to remain at the helm, having clocked up a total of 456 years - and long may they continue to so do.

ACKNOWLEDGEMENTS

Brian Pinfield was invaluable to me in beavering away at source material whilst the usual gang have contributed greatly to this book. Amongst these are: Richard Joseph for his invaluable help and advice in respect of matters technical; Ted Spittles regarding the production and reproduction of maps & plans as well as design and layout; and Viv Grady ever at the console and printer. Professional and technical bodies and their staff without whom I would not have been able to complete the publication and to whom I am indebted for access to and use of maps, plans, photographs and archive material include: Stephen Brooks, Director of The D-Day Museum, Portsmouth; the Picture Post Collection; the Imperial War Museum; and Portsmouth Publishing & Printing Ltd, in the guise of The News.

Last, but not least, Ron Wallis is a near neighbour who has, in his own way, both encouraged and helped me in this endeavour. As a 19 year old L/Cpl in 4th Commando, he was a D-Day warrior, landing near Lion on the Queen Green sector of Sword Beach-head. He completed his service as a Colour Sergeant and is our very own 6th June village hero. Bert Tomlin, another Southwick 'old soldier', spent much of his war fighting backwards and forwards along North Africa and helping in the occupation of Athens. That as they say, is another story.

Whilst preparing earlier history books (referred to above), I met and became a good friend of Graham Bishop. He actively encouraged my efforts, but sadly passed away last year.

Those whom I have inadvertently omitted will no doubt bend my ear and I hope will accept my sincere apologies.

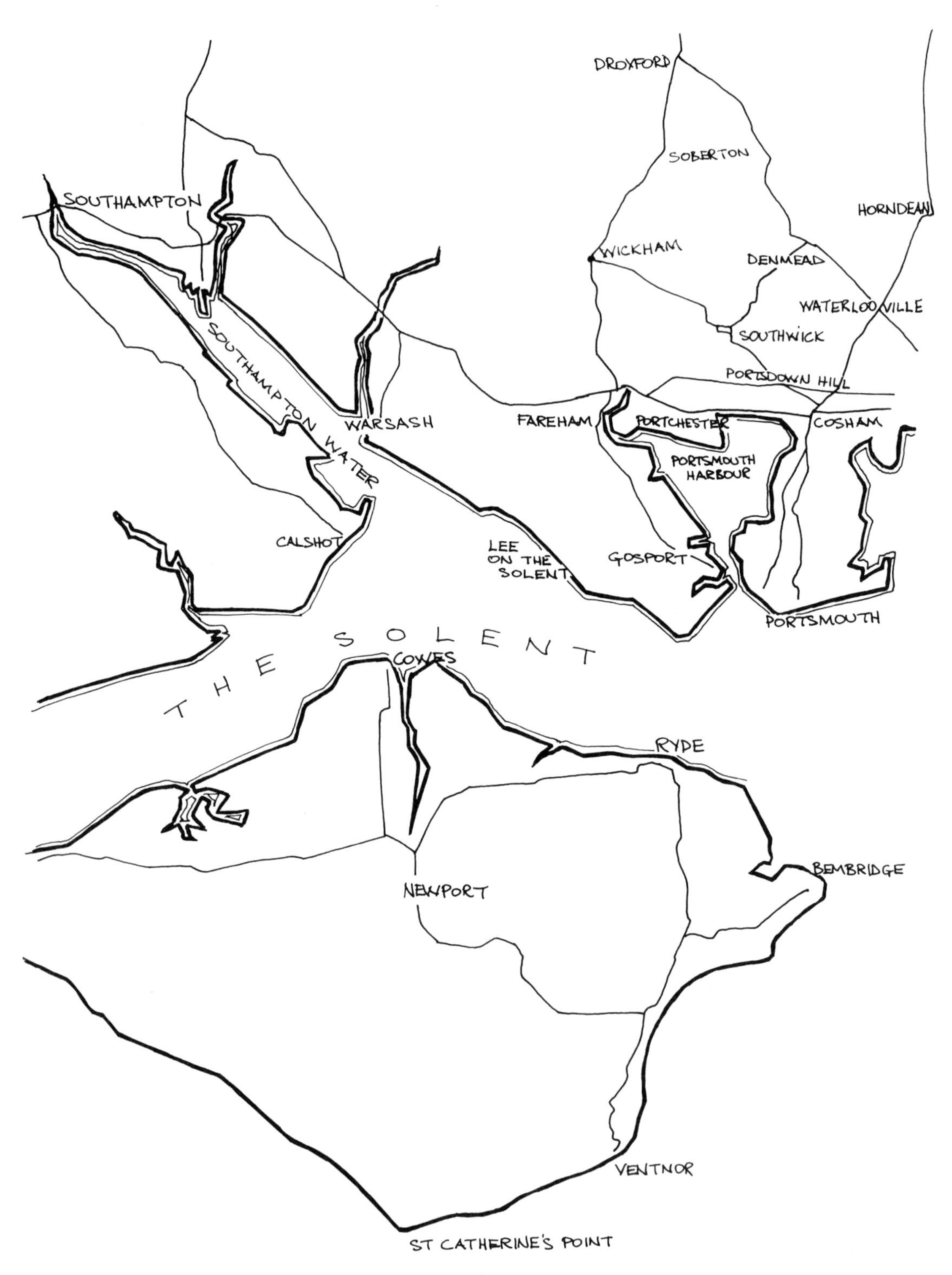

Illustration 1 The Area around Southwick

INTRODUCTION

The village of Southwick nestles at the south end of the Meon Valley, tucked into the foot of the north flank of Portsdown Hill (Illus 1 & 2). Present-day Estate holdings, even now spread out to Boarhunt, Cosham, Drayton, Fareham, Farlington, Paulsgrove, Portchester, Purbrook, Waterlooville, Widley and Wymering. It would be no exaggeration to label Southwick as a most unusual settlement which, throughout the last two millennium, has been, uniquely involved in the making of history.

Bronze Age

Early man settled in the area and pre-Bronze Age tribes peopled the Meon Valley and Portsdown Hill. Interesting flint implements are easily found on the local farmland and a number of Portsdown Hill barrows have been investigated. These include a Long Barrow to the east of the George Inn, where the old A3 cut through the crest of the hill, excavated in 1817. This yielded 12 skeletons, one of which had an arrowhead through its skull and was attributed to the Neolithic period, which ended about 2000BC.

Iron Age

Other excavations have revealed Bronze (2000-1000BC) and Iron Age (1000BC-AD0) burial areas. The Bronze Age dig was alongside the large roundabout at the top of the B2177* and the Iron Age excavation also beside the George Inn.

The Romans

Sleepy, enigmatic and secretive Southwick may have been, but its inhabitants were no strangers to conflict. The Romans' mighty war machine ploughed its way through the village in AD 43. They built a road (which they called Route 421) from Chichester in the east, via Havant, through Southwick, where they built a staging post, and on to Wickham. There the road divided, one branch leading to their naval base of Bitterne, the other to the major Roman city of Winchester. The pattern of thoroughfares included a link with their fort at modern-day Portchester. The Romans were followed by the battling, tribal Jutes and Meonwares. Incidentally, in 1066 the savage Normans probably used the very same Roman road in their conquest of Britain.

The Normans

The need for fortifications was not a strange concept to Southwick. Prior to the Norman invasion, the Saxons raised a number of earthwork forts around the village. These were probably part of a defensive network radiating out from Portchester Castle, which they had appropriated. Some 1,000 years later, as a result of the French invasion scares of the 1850/60s, a Southwick Lord of the Manor, Thomas Thistlethwayte (the younger), sold 900

**Incidentally, the Wickham-Southwick-Cosham road numbering varies. Sometimes it is A333, sometimes B2177 - it all depends if the local authorities and or highway chappies wish to duck spending money on its upkeep. No funds and it becomes a 'B' road. money spare and suddenly it is an 'A' thoroughfare!*

Illustration 2 Southwick Village and Surrounds

acres of Portsdown Hill to the Government, in 1862. The price was the then enormous sum of £95,200. Admittedly this princely sum took in the right to clear-fell the wooded hillsides in order to give an unimpeded field of fire. This explains the bare slopes. The land was required to construct a ring of hill-top defences. These included the Forts of Nelson, Purbrook, Southwick and Widley, as well as the Spithead Forts. They were nicknamed Palmerston's Follies, after the Prime Minister who pioneered the plan. The sobriquet Folly is not surprising as the feared invasion by the French did not materialise and never a shot was fired in anger!

Portsdown Hill

Palmerston's Follies

Invasion forces and their scheming generals were no stranger to Southwick. The Priory, the grounds and possessions, which were later to form the nucleus of Southwick Estate, played host to Edward III in the 1340s. That was when he launched his son, The Black Prince, and his troops on their initial forays into France, during the 100 Years War.

The Priory

Edward III & The Black Prince

Billeted soldiers were no stranger to Southwick. In the 1640s the Lord of Southwick Estates was the Parliamentarian 'Idle Dick' Norton. The 'idle' was reputably due to his disinclination to settle down to one task at a time. Be that as it may, he based his foot and horse troops, 'The Hambledon Boys', at Southwick during the Civil War battles, that tore England apart.

'Idle Dick' Norton

The Civil War

Royalty were no strangers to Southwick, as the village had played host to seven Kings of the Realm up until 1943.

Royal Visitors

Keeping secrets and being secretive was no strange experience for Southwick. These characteristics dated from the establishment of the all powerful, wealthy Southwick Priory, in about 1148. This medieval religious order controlled the area for some 400 years. The Priors and Canons were followed by a dynastic, influential, if reserved and taciturn family who took over many of the Priory's holdings. They were to remain at the helm, as private and self-contained as ever, until the outbreak of the Second World War (and on to this very day). From 1940 secrecy was the nation's watchword - 'Careless Talk Costs Lives'. But whatever was happening up at Southwick House, in the dark days of 1944, was the best kept secret of all. A rigid curtain of mystery was pulled tight around the building and its grounds - and no wonder. The family mansion had been chosen as the headquarters for the planning and execution of the greatest seaborne invasion the World had ever seen - the D-Day landings. From what had been the library, the Supreme Allied Commander was to issue the momentous order that triggered deployment of the massive forces which were to breach the Germans' Atlantic sea-wall defences, bring about the collapse of the once all-conquering Third Reich and end in the destruction of Hitler's Nazi war machine, in the bomb-torn bunkers of Berlin. That secretive and unique!

Southwick Priory

Illustration 3 Southwick and The Mansion in the 1930s

Chapter 1

The Village Prior To The War

The 1930s

The Squire's Unpreparedness

The outbreak of the Second World War, found the Squire of Southwick Mansion (Illus 3), which dominated the sleepy, secretive village, more than a little unprepared for the momentous events that were to alter his family destiny forever. To write a 'little' unprepared is a gross understatement of the facts! To be frank, the feudal village was still wedded to the 18thC, let alone the 19thC. For a start, it was owned lock-stock-and-barrel by the Squire, a 'lock-stock' which included the Church, St James Without The Priory Gates, both pubs and the nearby hamlet of South Boarhunt. In 1939 the Lord of the Manor was one Col Evelyn Thistlethwayte, whose family had enjoyed an unbroken suzerainty at Southwick Park and the surrounding 8000 acres or so for some 400 years. In fact, this ownership stretched back to the Dissolution of the Monasteries, an act of wanton robbery and destruction presided over by Henry VIII. The losers were the Priors and Canons of Southwick Priory, dispossessed in 1538. Now, all that remains of the once rich and wealthy St Augustine religious order of Black Canons, or secular priests, is a chunk of walling and the remains of a medieval pond.

Dissolution of the Monasteries

There was little contact between the villagers, who were almost all employees of the Estate and lived in tied cottages, and their lord and master. Until the mid 1930s, what communication took place was relayed by the Land Steward and or the Vicar, both also in the employ of the Squire. In the case of the Vicar this was a rather unique state of affairs due to the Church of St James Without The Priory Gates being a 'peculiar' and in the gift of the Estate owner, not the local Bishop. This rare state of affairs dated back to the various grants made to the Priory between 1133 and 1536.

The 'Peculiar'

The apparently cosy alliance of villager and squirearchy, living side by side, was in fact a very uneasy relationship. The various

The year is the Coronation of King George VI, 1937. To celebrate this propitious event, the patriotic Squire of Southwick, Col Evelyn Thistlethwayte, decided to plant a sapling oak in the corner of Oak Meadow. Here he is addressing 'his congregation' of loyal villagers.

PRIVATE COLLECTION

The Colonel planting the Coronation Oak, assisted by Mr Craig, the head forester.

PRIVATE COLLECTION

Lords of the Manor, who succeeded each other from 1900, rather in the style of *Kind Hearts & Coronets*, were fanatical sportsmen and very jealous of the estate covers which swarmed with game and bird. This combination of proximity and 'pot-worthiness' was to prove irresistible to the worthy artisans, who often poached for all they were worth. This latter proclivity proved to be extremely irritating to the occupants of the 'Big House' who, as local Justices of the Peace, had been transporting men for similar offences - only a hundred years previously. It shall be seen how the comparatively insignificant pheasant (insignificant except to other pheasants) was, indirectly, to play an eventful role in the waging of the coming war, more especially the D-Day landings, and were to have a catastrophic effect on the future of the Estate's property holdings. All will become plain!

The Insignificant Pheasant

Autocracy was a hallmark of the family and even as late as the 1930s woe betide anyone who failed to show their face during Sunday church services. Those without a satisfactory reason might well be hauled into the office to stutter their way through this or that explanation.

Col Evelyn Thistlethwayte

Col Evelyn Thistlethwayte had 'done his bit' for King and Country in various Colonial and European conflicts. His military activities included service in the South African Wars, between 1880-81 & 1899-1902, during which he was wounded twice and mentioned in dispatches, and the First World War. The Boer War woundings may be related to the possibly apocryphal story in which it was said that the Colonel received a bullet in his behind, a shot from one of the enemy guns. At a later date, whilst crawling towards the Boer lines, he was unfortunate to receive yet another 'posterior hit'. To everyone's surprise and horror he leapt up and, shaking his fist in the direction of the opposing forces, exclaimed "Damn you sir, that's the second time you've done that"! Duty done, he resigned his commission in the Kings Royal Rifle Corps to pursue the self-indulgent pursuits of following the horses, hunting and fishing. This involved spending the summer months at his town address of 3 Down Street, London WI, or one of his London Clubs -*The Carlton*, *Arthurs* or the *Naval and Military*. In stark contrast, the winter months were spent at Southwick Park in pursuit of both the eatable and uneatable.

The First World War

The First World War did not have a great impact on the Estate, its owners or the villagers. One immediate effect was that the 'resident' doctor left to 'join up'. He was the much respected Dr Balthazar, who lived and held surgery in South Lodge, as had the previous incumbents. Southwick was never again to enjoy the luxury of a 'live-in' village medico. The other side of Portsdown Hill was Queen Alexandra's Hospital which was a military facility. A Zeppelin raid on Portsmouth was reported as 'causing a little excitement'. The

A Zeppelin Raid

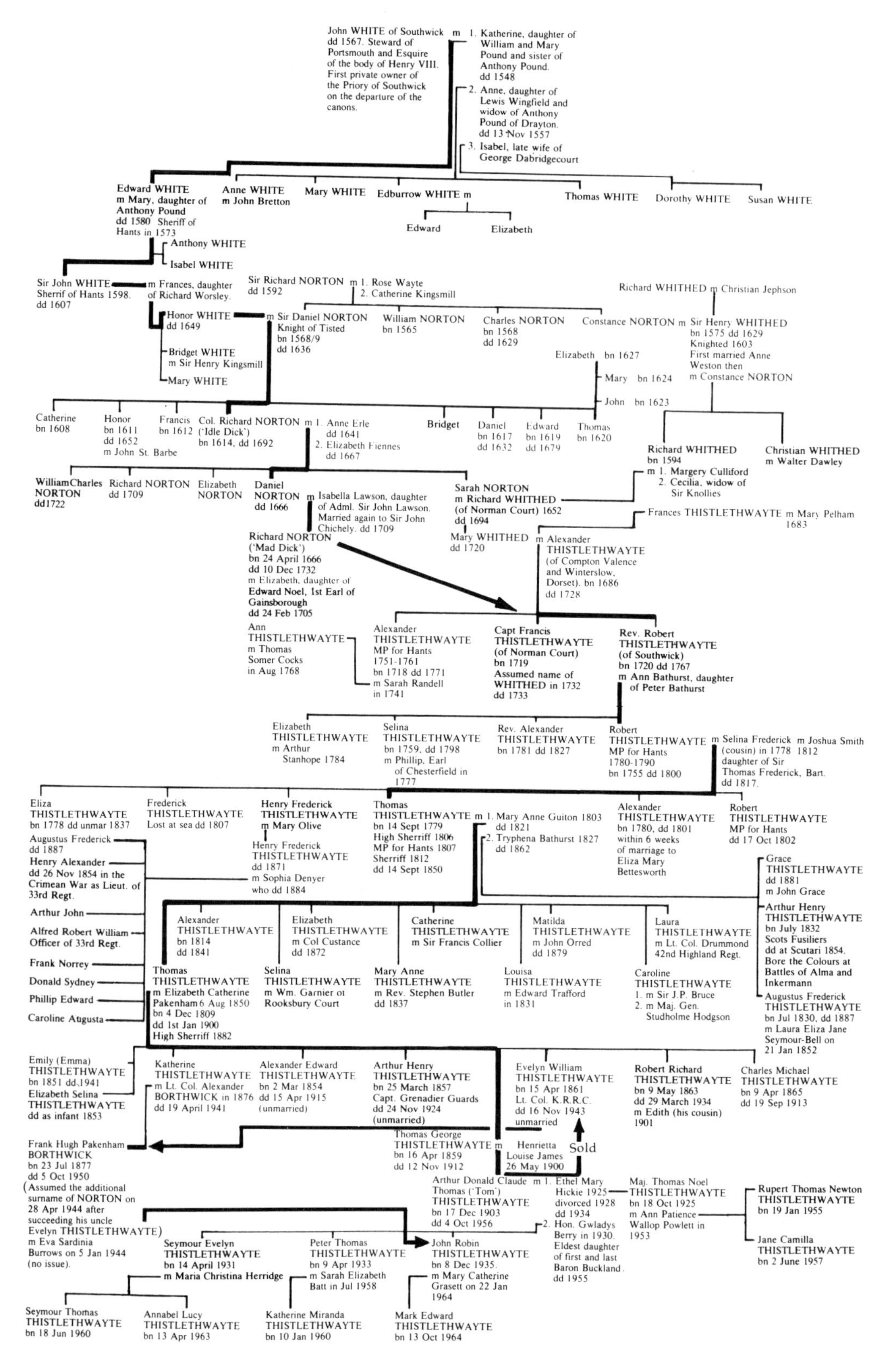

Illustration 4 The Thistlethwayte Inheritance

dirigible was supposedly clearly visible in the searchlights to all the inhabitants of the surrounding area. In those far off days the experience must have had a *War of the Worlds* impact. Another First World War loss was a golf course. This stretched along the south side of Portsdown Hill, from the club house beneath Fort Widley, towards New Barns farm, and back again. Perhaps the Zeppelin frightened the members away!

Mention of one of the hill-top forts reminds me that, at the outbreak of the Great War, they were utilised as assembly points for some of the regiments of horse-drawn heavy artillery, prior to embarkation for France. Amongst these, and best known to the villagers, was the 35th Battery. It should come as no surprise that the requisitioning of local horses did touch upon the community. The presence of army 'animal press gangs' resulted in both patronage of the village pubs and many attempts to pass-off useless nags. It is rumoured that the then Squire, Mr Alex, caused his finest mount to be secreted away, until after cessation of the recruitment drive.

Southwick Fair

Southwick Fair, held annually on the village green on the 6th April, was yet another casualty of the onset of hostilities, never to recommence. To accommodate the full panoply of a fair with all its various attractions and sideshows, the comparatively tiny greensward was supplemented by the use of the length of the High St. This was not difficult as the traffic in those days was sparse. In fact, it was restricted to the occasional horse-drawn farmer's wagon, the Portsmouth United Brewery dray, delivering to the Red Lion, or the carts of local carriers. In respect of the latter, apart from Portsmouth or Hambledon based firms, a village service was run by Billy Ainsworth. There were only three automobiles within the bounds of the village. These were in the ownership of Capt Long, residing at Oak Lodge and of Long's Brewery (Portsmouth) fame, Mr Morgan, the Estate Steward, domiciled in Bridge House, and Dr Balthazar of South Lodge. The latter vehicle was a three wheeler steered by the use of a tiller. Not surprisingly, considering their 'reluctance' to come to terms with the modern world, the incumbents of the 'Big House' had not aspired to possession of an internal combustion driven, horseless conveyance. The Squires were to remain faithful to a brougham and dog cart for many years to come.

The Village Carriers

The Path of Inheritance

Perhaps one of the strangest twists in this story of Southwick and its extraordinary role in the theatre of the Second World War is not that Robin Thistlethwayte, the present owner of the Estate, is the great nephew of Col Evelyn. Oh no! The fascinating twist of fate is in the path of inheritance - more a maze really (Illus 4).

The Mansion Staff

In the 1930s, the Colonel and some close family lived at Southwick House. They were looked after by a 'modest' retinue of servants which took in a coachman, chauffeur, a head gardener and his team,

The original village Post Office, at about the turn of the century. (The Red Lion is 'off camera' at the left of the terrace).
PRIVATE COLLECTION

A view of the Golden Lion, with The Mansion's market garden wall in the background, and a vintage vehicle trundling down towards Rook's Bridge.
PRIVATE COLLECTION

The Village School and, in the background, The Mansion's main lodge gates, with the Church on the right-hand side of the picture.
PRIVATE COLLECTION

a head gamekeeper and his lads, a head housemaid and her help, a housekeeper, two butlers, a stable boy and an odd job man. These were in addition to the Estate staff, comprising an agent, bailiff, clerk, foreman and foresters, and the Vicar. In fact the Mansion was rented from Col Evelyn's nephew, Arthur Donald Claude Thistlethwayte, nicknamed Tom. The latter had become owner on the death of his uncle Arthur Henry, in 1924. Tom's father was Captain Thomas George, Royal Artillery, and mother Henrietta Louise James, an actress. Their marriage, in 1900, had caused quite a 'stir' in the family, but the bold Captain was not to inherit, as he passed away in 1912. Son Arthur, born in 1903 and one time racing driver, popularly known as Tom, did not make Southwick his residence, preferring to let the property. Without doubt, Tom was a charming, urbane gentleman but is reported to have been rather ungracious on inheriting the Estate. He is supposed to have commented, at the reading of the Will and on hearing of his share "That it was not enough to buy a breakfast with"! It must have been a big breakfast! Tom inherited at the tender age of 21 and first married the daughter of an Irish Colonel when he was 22. By the time he was 25 he was divorced and had married the Hon Gwladys Berry, eldest daughter of the first and last Baron Buckland, when he was 27. This lady was mother to three sons, the youngest of which is John Robin 'T', the present Squire.

'Tom' Thistlethwayte

During his tenure as owner of the Southwick Estates, Tom embarked on a series of property disposals, supposedly to keep finances on an even keel. Amongst the placings, Portchester Castle was passed over to the Ministry of Works, under a deed of Guardianship, and Hipley Farm, adjacent to the Horse and Jockey Pub, was sold. Meantime engulfed in a time-warp, Tom's jovial uncle, Col Evelyn and his diminutive, shortsighted sister Miss Emily (Emma) rented the Mansion and Park, Wanstead Farm and the Estate's shooting rights. Miss Emily well represented the eccentricities of that generation of the family. She died in 1941, aged 90, and dressed all her life in an early Victorian style - bonnet, bustles, *et al,* and peered at the world through a lorgnette. Ensconced with them in the Big House was brother Robert, known as Robin. He had married a cousin but, being a dedicated hunting and fishing man, lived in the Mansion, visiting his wife at their London home once or twice a year. The amazing *menage a trois* was sometimes joined by a widowed sister, Katherine. She had married a Lt Col Alexander Borthwick, owner of Scottish Estates and the Glenfiddich whisky distillery. Their offspring, Frank Hugh Pakenham Borthwick, was to inherit the Estate from Col Evelyn Thistlethwayte. A widowed sister-in-law of Katherine was another house guest.

Disposals

The Resident Family

Retrograde as the property sales may have seemed to Tom's elderly relations residing in the 'Big House', who believed in adding to

The Village pump and Green from the Church end...
PRIVATE COLLECTION

...and from the Golden Lion.
PRIVATE COLLECTION

A view of the junction of Back Lane and the High St, with the road to Denmead curving away round the wall of Castle Farm.
PRIVATE COLLECTION

the Estate, not selling off bits and pieces, a worse, much worse scenario was to unfold. When Tom inherited the Colonel was aged 63. He, his close family and their servants were well happy in the splendid Southwick Mansion encircled by its walled parkland. Here they were cocooned from the outside world, from the advances and inexorable social changes of the 1930s, by a very Victorian attitude of mind and the cushion of vast personal wealth, coupled with the comparative isolation offered by the Estate. The prospect of this hedonistic way of life, this comfortable and cosy arrangement, which had lasted for years, continuing until the end of their days was critically endangered when it became apparent that Tom was contemplating selling off the Estate - lock, stock and 'pheasant covey'. This calamity became a distinct possibility with the arrival on the scene of a wealthy South African racehorse owner, 'Solly Joe', who was a serious contender to make the purchase.

'Tom' Considers Selling Up

Let it not be said that redoubtable Col Evelyn had lost any of his pioneering, thrusting spirit. After a lot of soul-searching and probably much gentlemanly swearing, in about 1931 he stumped up. He purchased the whole 'shooting match' from Young Tom, placing it in older, more conservative family hands. Mind you, the acquisition was not made without some inconvenience for the Colonel was forced to sell some London real estate in order to 'raise the wind' for the transaction. In fact it must have rankled not a little, for when the deal was done, Col Evelyn called together all the tenant farmers and gave them an ear pounding. I'm not quite sure why, unless the tirade preceded a rent rise, but in the course of the one-sided chat, the bemused farmers were advised that he, the Colonel, 'had been forced to sell property in London, earning ten to twelve percent, in order to buy this lot, which only earns two per cent'! As if in punishment, for so inconveniencing his uncles and aunts, who at the very best considered him a spendthrift, Tom's inheritance, if not his very existence, was ignored in later years. Certainly the various family genealogists seemed to be unaware of him.

The Colonel Purchases

Whatever, that should have settled matters, for at least Evelyn's lifetime. Unfortunately, events elsewhere in Europe were taking a tragic turn which, ultimately, were to uproot the family from its outmoded time capsule. The fascinating consideration is that if Tom had not been so disinterested in his inheritance, part of the D-Day history might have been written quite differently. If Uncle Evelyn had not been forced to purchase the Estate, to protect his and his immediate relations way of life, the seeds of the loss of the Mansion and its Park may not have been sown. Even Hitler might not have succeeded in disturbing the archaic state of affairs, had the Colonel not unwittingly given fate a helping hand - in the shape of his previously referred to pheasants. They were to prove to be Southwick's Trojan Horse.

The Trojan Horse

What is a Steam Brewery?
PRIVATE COLLECTION

Facing up the High St, with South Lodge on the right.
PRIVATE COLLECTION

The Red Lion is in the background, to the right. The flag flying from the upper window probably indicates a public holiday of some sort.
PRIVATE COLLECTION

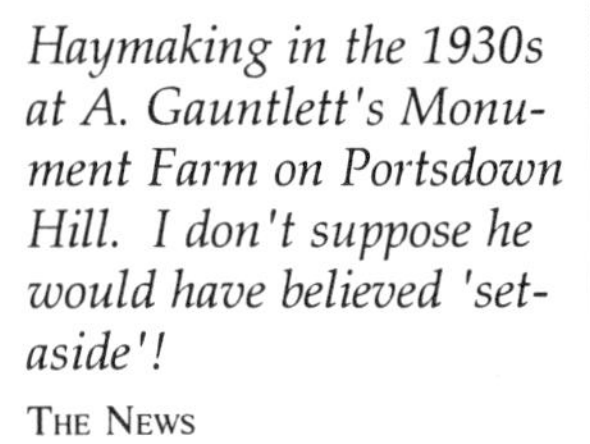

Haymaking in the 1930s at A. Gauntlett's Monument Farm on Portsdown Hill. I don't suppose he would have believed 'set-aside'!
THE NEWS

Chapter 2

The Village Goes To War

1940

Immediately after the outbreak of the Second World War, Col Evelyn was in the habit of offering a gun on the Estate's shoot to an Admiral Sir William James. He was the Naval Commander in Chief at Portsmouth. The Admiral, who later was to accept some of the blame for the Navy requisitioning Southwick Mansion, sets the scene and atmosphere of the time in the following extracts, the first from his book *The Sky Was Always Blue* published by Metheun, London and the others from *The Portsmouth Letters* published by Macmillan.

Admiral James Gets A Gun In The Door

'I had always been accustomed to taking exercise every day and during the previous summer I had kept fit by walking along the top of Portsdown Hill every afternoon, but just when I was getting rather bored with this walk Col Thistlethwayte invited me to a day's shooting on the reverse side of the hill. That was the beginning of a remarkable shooting season ... I owe a great debt to the Colonel. The sirens were screeching nearly every night that winter (*in Portsmouth*) and there was no better refreshment to body and mind than an hour or two in the country with keepers who still thought in terms of wildlife and talked of the habits of birds and animals instead of the habits of Hitler and his gangsters.'

The Admiral Goes Shooting

'25 Sept 1940. ...I am keeping very fit, thanks to old Col Thistlethwayte of Southwick Park. He owns about 8000 acres just over Portsdown Hill, and has told his keeper to arrange the shooting with me. Its a gift from the Gods. We only shoot for 2 hrs at a time, and I slip away after I have done my papers and correspondence, arrive at the first stand 20 minutes later, and get back from lunch. Fogg-Elliot, my Flag Lieutenant, is a keen shot and he and I, and sometimes one other, are going to go twice a week. There are any number of birds in the covers and I look forward to some grand sport, if my name is not on a bomb. We got 39 pheasants and 4 brace of partridge pottering on the outside yesterday. That will make your mouth water.'

'28th Oct 1940. ... at Southwick we are averaging over 50 pheasants a

Enlisting for the war at Portsmouth in 1940...
THE NEWS

...and squeezing into the new boots at Cosham. Wait until they have to iron the toecaps with hot spoons!
THE NEWS

'Blowing up' a barrage balloon at Portchester. The fact that the chaps appear to be weighted down a bit, by all that clothing, is - because they are kitted out with anti-gas gear!
THE NEWS

> session (2 hrs). This morning 3 of us shot 73, and we are only allowed one gun. Its saving my life.'
>
> '25th Dec 1940. 'I am still at old Thistlethwayte's pheasants, always the 2 hour sessions and always 50-60 (birds). They are getting more difficult now. I have also had a good day at Idsworth, Lorna Howe's place near Horndean; we got 110.'
>
> '1st Feb 1941. Despite all my preoccupation, I have managed to slip in some good days at Southwick. Three of us got 89 birds in the first 2 hours on the 23rd (January). That is our best so far, a good best you will agree.'
>
> '20th Feb 1941. Alas, shooting is over. Believe me, or believe me not, three of us got 71 pheasants on Feb 1st, our last 2 hour session. It has been an amazing season. The total bag was 1450. Now I must take to hiking again on Portsdown Hill.'

The Cuckoo Settles

In giving the Admiral the run of his shoot, unbeknowingly Col Evelyn encouraged a cuckoo to settle comfortably in the Southwick nest, he drew a Trojan Horse into Park. The intruder? That was to be the Royal Naval School of Navigation. At the outbreak of war the 'Navigators' were located in the Portsmouth Dockyard shore base *HMS Dryad*. The latter was named after a twin screw gunboat, built in 1893, and the fourth ship of that name allocated to the school when they were given dry land facilities, in 1906. On 11th July 1940 the Dockyard experienced its first air raid, with a second on the 24th July. From then on irregular attacks were endured for the remainder of the year. The Navigation School's buildings were especially susceptible to fire so it was necessary to organize night patrols, which had to be drawn from the teachers and students. Naturally, these extra curricula activities effected the ability of staff and pupils alike, and resulted in a fairly tired set of chaps, many unable to stop falling asleep during lectures. The base Captain mentioned the problem to Admiral James who, in turn, persuaded the good Colonel, early in 1941, to allow the officer pupils to spend their nights at Southwick House. The cuckoo was laying its egg, the Trojan Horse had entered the walls!

The Egg is Laid The Trojan Horse Rumbles In

Even at Southwick, air raid sirens caused the officers to retreat to the cellars to complete their nights' sleep. Vice Admiral Schofield relates a number of first-hand accounts of these trying times from the diaries of Admiral James, including the following memories of a Capt R H Graham*.

> 'One night when the sirens had sounded, we dutifully descended to the cellars for shelter. After a lapse of half an hour, during which nothing

* *With acknowledgements to 'Navigation and Direction The story of HMS Dryad' by Vice Admiral B B Schofield, published by Kenneth Mason, Emsworth.*

Early-day evacuees depart Portsmouth for the delights of the IOW, the Meon Valley or more distant parts of Hampshire. Note the labels. Probably their gloves and mittens were secured with elastic and string threaded up and over their coat arms - if my memory is accurate.

THE NEWS

Anxious mums oversee the enforced separation from their children.

THE NEWS

One of the destinations for evacuees was South Harting, which appears to have altered very little.

THE NEWS

happened to disturb our peace, there was a sudden clatter in the cellar. We looked up to see Col Thistlethwayte appear clad in a heavy woollen dressing gown and seated in a wheelchair, being propelled by two menservants. He was protesting loudly at being dragged down to the basement at that hour of the night. On another occasion, we awoke early one morning and, looking out of our bedroom window, across the park saw the white tresses of a parachute entangled in a magnificent oak tree on the edge of the lawn to the south of [*Southwick*] the house. Ah, we thought, a filthy hun who had been... shot down by our... night fighters. We assumed the dark shape at the end of the harness must be his body hanging still and lifeless. Ought we to go and cut him down, and report our action to the Commander in Chief's office? On closer inspection the dangling shape appeared too regular to be that of a body. Then the awful truth dawned on us; it was a land mine which had failed to explode - as yet! We washed and dressed, returning to the Navigation School (in Portsmouth) for breakfast and subsequently heard, that the bomb disposal experts came later and removed the offending object.

Parachute Silk and Ladies Underwear

The above story in respect of the land mine is well remembered by a local lady, still a village resident but then a young bar assistant at the Golden Lion pub. She was given a length of the parachute cord (by one of the officers), which sits close by me as I relate these words. She and the other village lasses gladly shared out amongst themselves the silk parachute material which was quickly machined into glamorous underwear. Most welcome in those far-off days of clothing coupons and rationing. Need a chap say more?

The Dockyard Is Bombed

Events were now gathering pace, unbeknown to Col Thistlethwayte. In March 1941, the Navigation School suffered a direct hit, but continued operating until sustaining even more serious damage to its surrounds, in the months of April and May. Incidentally, during these selfsame raids over Portsmouth a land mine landed fairly close to Southwick, in nearby Creech Woods. It blasted a large crater, still visible to this day, if water filled.

The Cuckoo's Egg Hatches

The exact date that the cuckoo's egg hatched, that the men of the Navigation School upped sticks from Portsmouth and spilled out of the Trojan Horse to engulf Southwick House and its grounds appears not to have been logged. Vice Admiral Schofield* records that Admiral James, in his diary of the 22nd May 1941 writes:

'I am glad to say the Navigation School will move shortly to Southwick'.

It is recorded elsewhere that it was not until the 27th September 1941 that the change of residence was finalized. Whenever, Admiral James, in another extract from *The Portsmouth Letters* published by

* *With acknowledgements to 'Navigation and Direction The story of HMS Dryad' by Vice Admiral B B Schofield, published by Kenneth Mason, Emsworth.*

Southwick House about the time of its requisition by the navy in 1941.
HMS DRYAD

The destruction of Southwick House stables, to make way for the Action Information Training Centre (AITC), in about 1943.
HMS DRYAD

The old boy might have been the family groom.
HMS DRYAD

Macmillan, recorded:

> '12th Nov 1941. ... but alas no more of those wonderful 2 hour sessions at Southwick. The house was taken for the Navigation School, and old 'T' looks on me now as a double-dyed villain, and not a fit person to shoot his birds.'

The Colonel was simply staggered. His family and ancestors had owned Southwick Mansion and the surrounding lands for some 400 years. Through good husbandry, guile and some subterfuge; sometimes via the female line, the Whites, Nortons and Thistlethwaytes had not only clung on, but added to and consolidated the Estate. And this, despite periods of eccentricity, some lassitude, self-indulgence, untimely death and wildly changing social conditions. In fact, due to the excellent stewardship of father and son Thomas Thistlethwayte, between 1800 and 1900, the Estate had expanded to include almost all the original possessions. These dated back to 1539 when John White purchased Southwick Priory and some of its lands from Thomas Wriothesley, Earl of Southampton. John White had been one of King Henry VIIIs architects of the Dissolution of the Monasteries in Hampshire.

Eviction!

It just was not fair! The old boy, the archetypal Colonel was being unceremoniously bundled out of the family home by the Navy. Not that he gave in easily. Prior to this eviction, Lt Col Evelyn William Thistlethwayte and his retinue of servants lurked around the perimeter of the Mansion and its cellars. The naval personnel lived in a state of uneasy truce with the Squire and his employees. Inevitably, after the Mansion and Park were official requisitioned, in 1942, they were forcibly ejected. This ended in a rather undignified scene, the Colonel being very reluctant to leave! At this time a number of the servants were 'put out to pasture' but to the very end the atmosphere 'downstairs' was as feudal as 'upstairs'. Even after he had left service, the butler, Mr Pettitt, insisted on dressing for dinner.

The Colonel Relocates

In these distressing circumstances, the Colonel was first relocated to Bridge House, on the corner of Back Lane and Bridge Street, but only after the agent, Mr Willoughby, had moved out. Much of the antique and monstrous old furniture from the Mansion was placed in store. The Colonel's Rolls Royce and the Estate's commercial lorry, a 1932 Morris, were pushed out of their garages by the Army. Harry Goodall had rejoined the Estate work-force in 1936 to be driver of this lorry. He was sent to Wadhams of Southsea (which was to become Wadham Stringer and eventually taken over by Kennings) for a couple of week's driving lessons, but even his illustrious employer could not save the lorry being used as a fowl house for a time. Harry is of the impression that the Army requisitioned

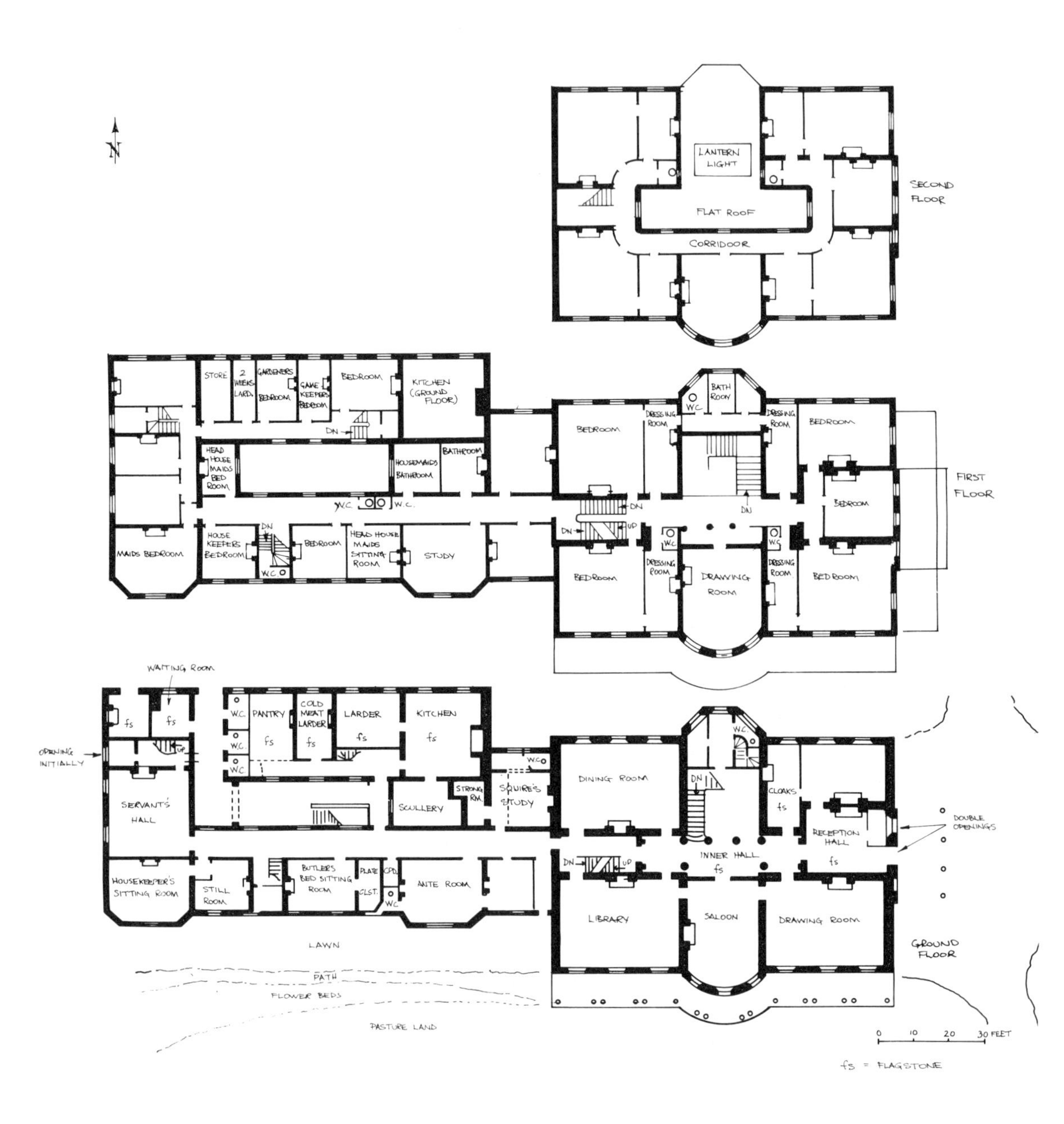

Illustration 5 Southwick Mansion, early 1943, prior to substantial alterations

part of the Mansion stables, before the Navy's arrival, to house the stores necessary to operate the gun batteries installed in The Park. There was a gun emplacement adjacent to Pinsley Lodge and another on 'The Slopes', with a total of 72 Bofors anti-aircraft guns.

The Park Gun Batteries

Having the Colonel domiciled in Bridge House was considered a little too close for comfort by Mr Willoughby. This impression was reinforced due to the Squire's habit of wandering over to the nearby Estate Laundry and chatting with the employees. I mean to say, you could never be sure what might come to light in these unmonitored exchanges. The Colonel was persuaded to move to Broomfield House, which was to become his final resting place.

The Colonel Moves Again

Confusingly, Admiral James is reported to have dairy noted yet again, but this time on the 12th November 1943, that there weren't any more pheasant shooting sessions and that Col Evelyn regarded him as a rotter, or words to that effect! Four days after that entry, on the 16th November I943, the anachronistic but splendidly courageous old gentleman, Lt Col Evelyn Thistlethwayte, KRRC and bachelor, passed away. He was aged 82 and the family lost the last direct line with the dynastic 18th & 19thC Thistlethwaytes. At his death, both the Mansion servants and Estate staff and employees attended the funeral. The coffin bearers included F Colwell, A Carter, A Faithful, J Squib, W Harefield and H Green. Also in attendance were C Willoughby (Agent), Miss M Scott (clerk), A S Faithful (foreman), T A Scott and F Cragg (foresters), J Painter (bailiff), A Cotrell (head gardener), F Wesley (head gamekeeper) Mrs Fletcher (housekeeper), Miss B Poole (head housemaid), J Pettitt and W Dunnett (butlers) and E A Thompson (chauffeur). No mention is made of a 'Gilbert', but he was head gardener and his family had been Estate gardeners for three generations. Other, unlisted staff included two more housemaids (one parlour, one scullery) and a kitchen-maid, as well as a stable boy and an odd job man, the latter domiciled in the stables.

The Colonel Passes On

Being unmarried and the last of the generation alive, inheritance followed the general thrust of the, by then, disbanded Family Trust. The Estate had been purchased from Tom, the issue of Evelyn's brother Thomas George, and now passed to the only other assignee alive, the son of Evelyn's sister Katherine, Frank Hugh Pakenham Borthwick. His father, Lt Col Borthwick, had married Katherine, sister of Alexander, Arthur and Evelyn. This change in direction of the inheritance coincided with the dawn of a new and starker era, hustled into being by the onset of the Second World War.

...& a Borthwick Inherits

The forcible requisitioning of Southwick House and the Park may well have hastened the death of the gallant Colonel. Strange to relate, the eventual compulsory purchase and the derisory price paid for the same property, in 1950, quite possibly contributed to the death of the Colonel's successor.

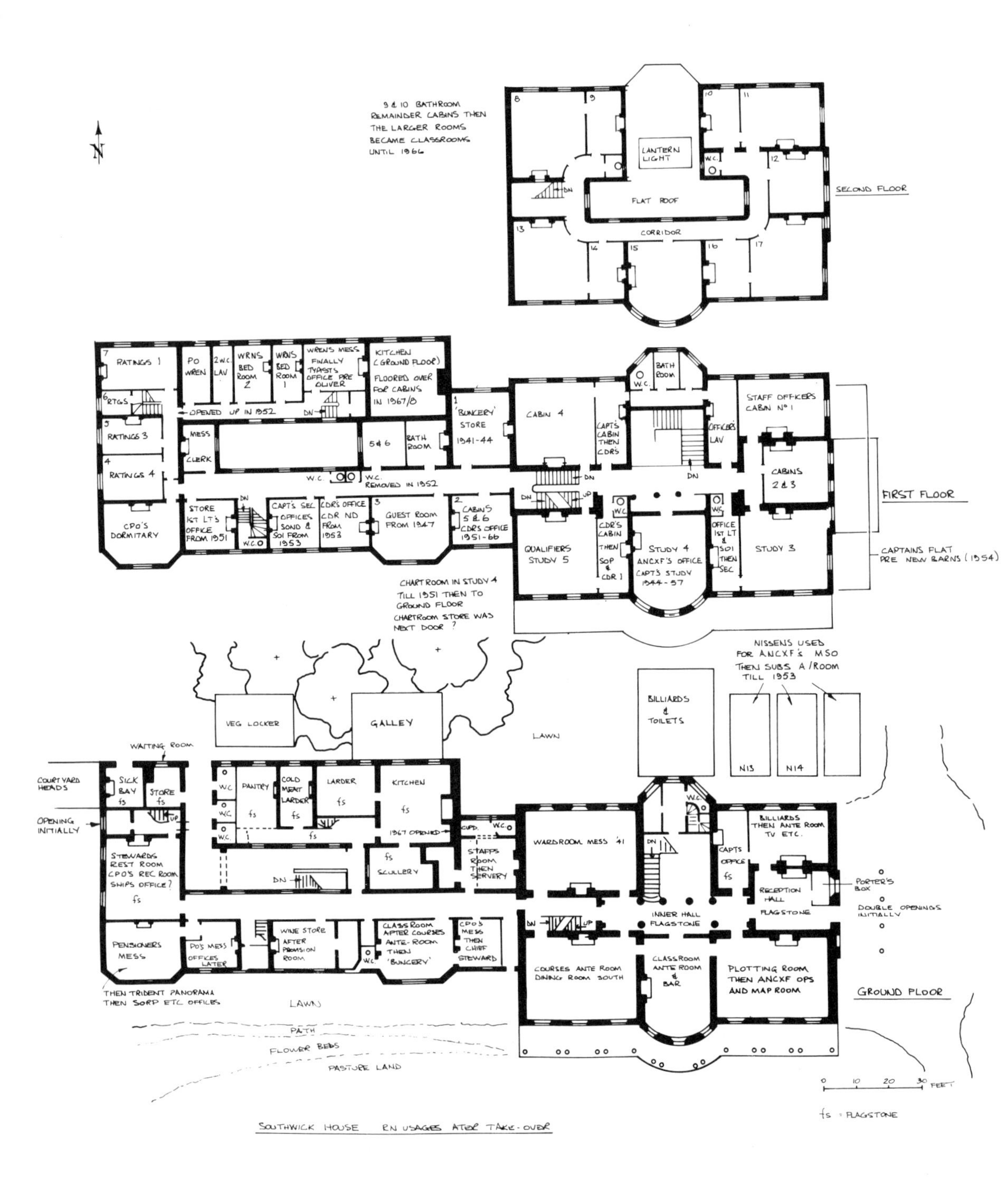

Illustration 6 Southwick Mansion, after the Naval Take-over and 'substantial alterations'.

CHAPTER 3

THE VILLAGE AT WAR

1943

Southwick & Invasions

It must not be thought that sleepy, secretive Southwick was a stranger to conflict, invasion forces or scheming generals. The launching of 'Operation OVERLORD' on the 6th June 1944, setting in motion the invasion of France and leading ultimately to the liberation of Europe, was simply history repeating itself. Some 488 or 499 years previously, Edward III, whilst staying at Southwick Priory, sent forth his son, the 'Black Prince' to invade France. It has to be accepted that this was to reinforce King Edward's claim to the Crown of France, not to relieve the country from an unwanted, oppressive invader.

The takeover of Southwick Mansion and Park by the Royal Naval Navigation School was a step taken on the retreat, as it were. Portsmouth, in common with many other English ports and cities was taking a pounding from German bombers. But even whilst Britain was involved in a life and death struggle to survive, during the first three years of the war, a planning group was in 'deep thought'. Set up as early as 1941, its members were dreaming up various schemes for the eventual invasion of Europe. The first of these plans was code-named ROUNDUP. By 1942, in order to help relieve the intolerable German forces' pressure on the Russians, a limited invasion, involving a bridgehead in France, was envisaged and code-named SLEDGE HAMMER. The entry of the United States of America into the war, coupled with the decision to liberate Europe prior to other long term objectives, enabled the planners to widen their invasion horizons. Their deliberations resulted in operation SUPER ROUNDUP originally conceived to be put into action in 1943. This optimistic schedule was inevitably subject to slippage and had to be abandoned. In January 1943 the Casablanca Conference (North Africa) was convened. It was attended by President Roosevelt and Prime Minister Winston Churchill and the decision was made to invade Northern France in May 1944, the overall operation being code-named OVERLORD.

ROUND UP

SLEDGE HAMMER

SUPER ROUNDUP

Casablanca Conference & OVERLORD

In the meantime, despite an admittedly limited number of military personnel present, few, if any, alterations had taken place to

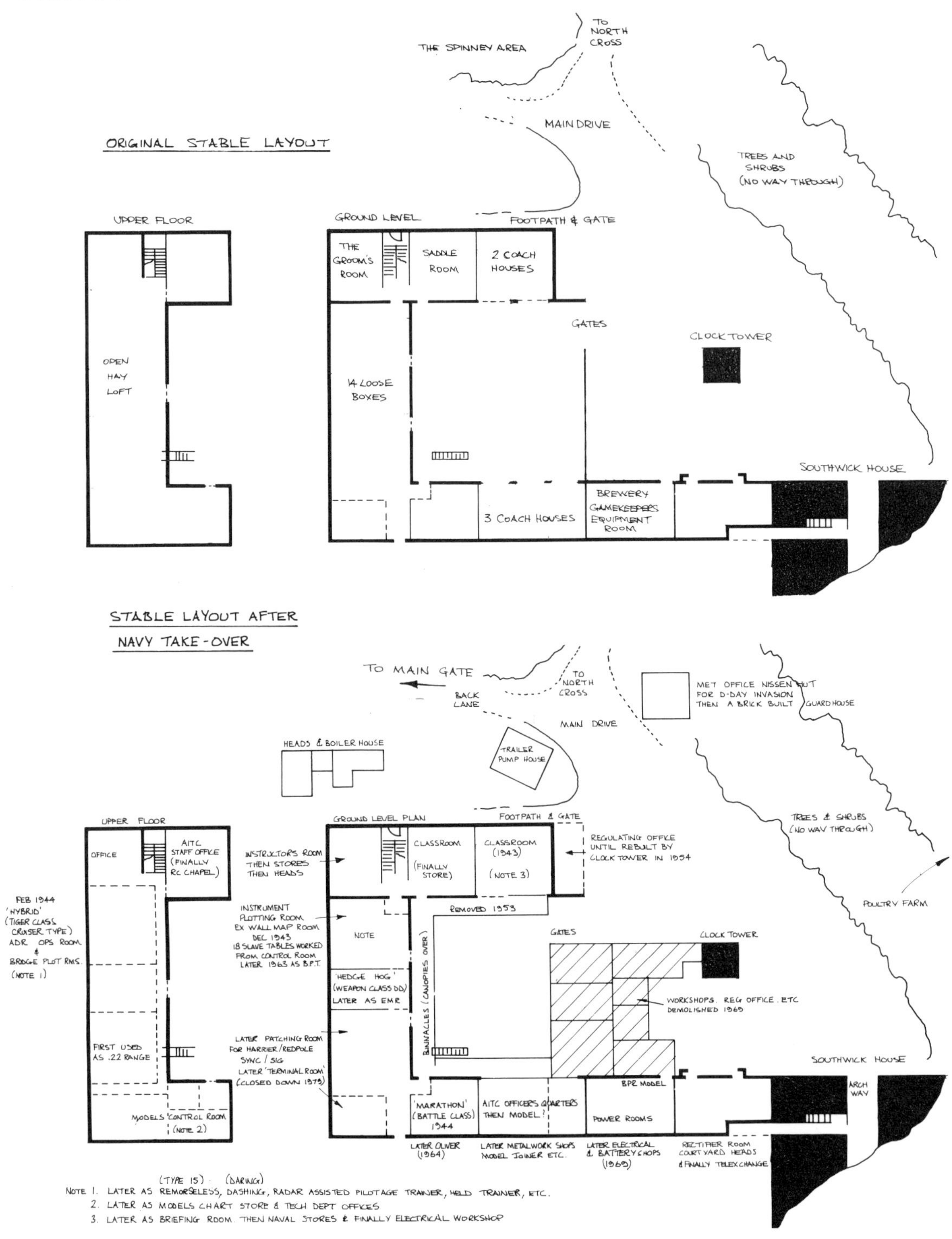

Illustration 7 Southwick Mansion Stables - before and after the Naval Take-over in 1943

Southwick Mansion, its surrounds and the Park (Illus 5 & 6). Three Nissen huts had been erected to the north side of the building, adjacent to the main entrance, and a poultry run installed in the Spinney. At the time of the takeover, the House had its own, ancient, oil-fired electricity generating plant and battery bank, located in some brick outbuildings on the drive edge of the Spinney. The water was drawn from a well and pumped up to roof tanks. Naturally, these limited services and supplies had to be supplemented and then replaced, but until the middle of 1943, no other structural changes took place. Meanwhile, in the village the ladies of the duty watch WRNS (Womens Royal Navy Service) were quartered in South Lodge, alongside the Golden Lion.

The Mansion & Stable Modifications

The month of June 1943 was when the 'modifications' commenced, with a vengeance. Conversion of the stable block was put in hand in order to make way for the 'Action Information Training Centre' (AITC). These alterations resulted in the stables being gutted and altered (Illus 7). The contractors complained that a 'resident' groom was living 'in unbelievable squalor'. This report conflicts with the acknowledged fastidiousness of the 'Brothers Thistlethwayte' (Alexander, Arthur and Evelyn). They were renowned for ensuring that the stables were kept in an absolutely immaculate condition. Alexander Edward, known as Alex, was renowned, in a family noted for their individuality, as a rather 'careful' eccentric. He is supposed to have saved pennies by repairing the holes in his incredibly old, mould green, mackintosh - with string. The servants were instructed to do the same with the mansion carpets. Alex did not usually rise until early afternoon and expected his pony and carriage to be ready 'prompt at 5 pm'. With coachman Boulter sitting behind, Alex would drive into Fareham to obtain 'half' an evening paper for a 1/2d, rather than pay a full penny for the cost of the whole edition. I suppose that is how a millionaire stays one. He returned, as regular as clockwork, at 6 pm. It was Alex who set the style for pinching out the candles in the drive, rather than keep them lit all the way up to the mansion doors. Squire Alex was fastidious and prior to mounting the carriage the rear of the pony was washed off. The stables also had to be kept spotless and any droppings there, or on the drive, immediately removed. Oddly enough, the carriage pony was hired from London, yet he purchased five or six horses, five polo ponies and a cob, which simply ran wild in the grounds of the Park. Probably, the 'stable state' on the Naval occupation was due to the confusion of the early war years, coupled with the upheavals and subsequent ousting of unsuspecting, hapless Col Evelyn.

Half A Paper For Half A Penny

WRNS' Dormitories

In the village, WRNS' sleeping quarters were erected in the gardens of South Lodge, resulting in the single storey, prefab-like building still in existence and now known, rather grandly, as the Manor

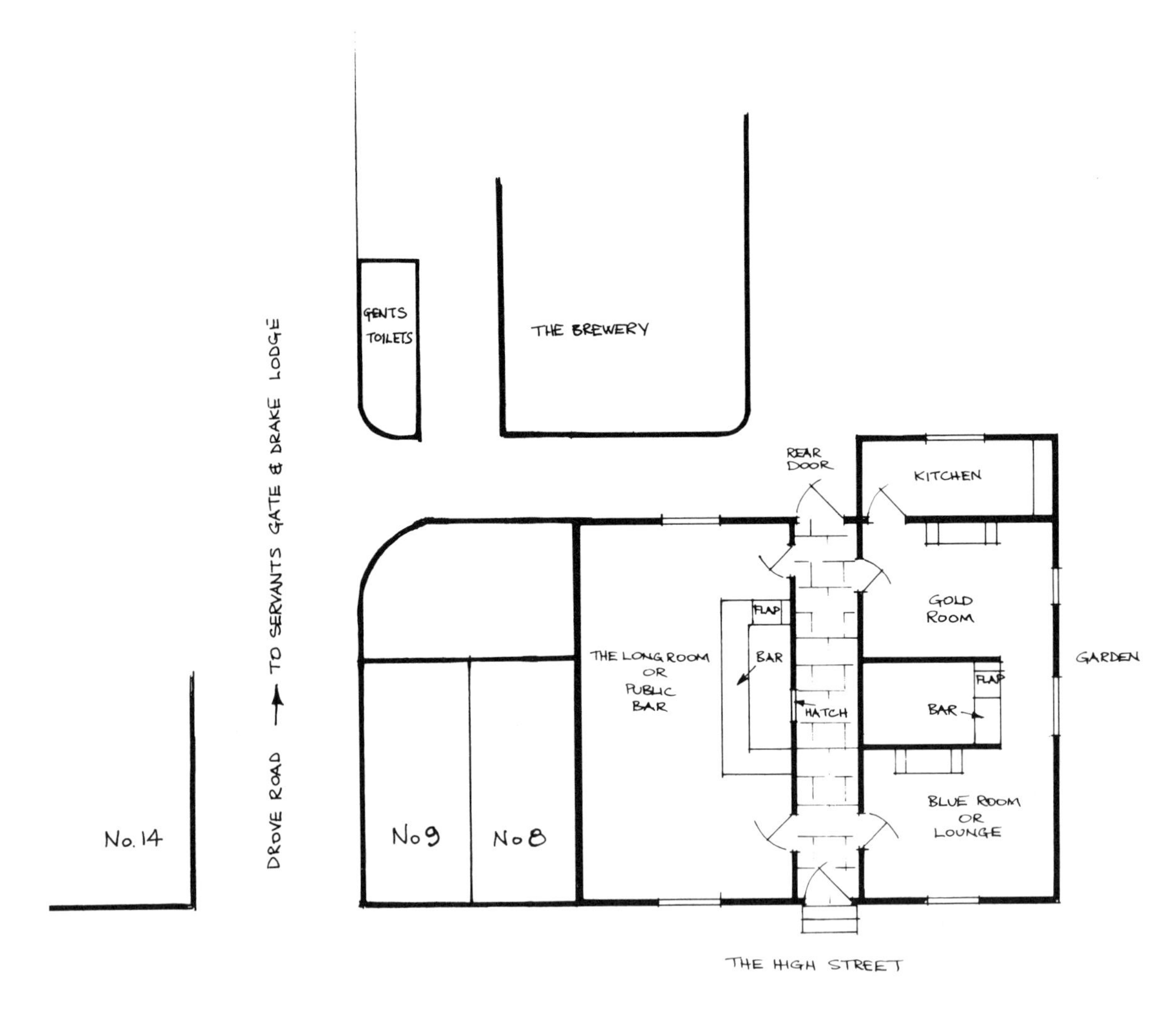

Illustration 8 The Wartime Golden Lion Layout

Hall. Considering the armed forces notoriety for 'improving' anything within their sphere of influence, posterity must be delighted that the latter is the only permanent monument to Ministry of Defence 'mutilation' perpetrated outside the walls of the Mansion and Park. Shelters were erected in the field beside the old Dower House, known as The Elms, and situated in West St. Their purpose was to temporarily house the schoolchildren during 1943, on those occasions when the School was commandeered by the Army for Staff planning meetings. Once Southwick House had been sufficiently altered to cater for most eventualities, these shelters were appropriated to provide even more WRNS' quarters.

In the main, village life remained remarkably unaffected. It would be strange to relate that the momentous changes taking place up at the Big House, with the resultant influx of service personnel, did not have some effect on the previously measured way of life. At first the locations at which the greatest impact was apparent were the two village pubs, the 'Red' and the 'Golden' Lions, where the increase in trade was extremely welcome. Apart from the Red Lion only being a beer house, a further disadvantage, shared with almost ever other pub in the Kingdom during the war, was the rationing restrictions which caused shortfalls in supplies. For reasons that will become clear, the other hostelry, the Golden Lion, did not suffer from such hindrances to its supplies. Thus, once the Navy had taken over Southwick Mansion, the 'Blue Room' lounge bar of the Golden was adopted as an unofficial officers mess. Actually this bar was divided into two - the 'Blue Room' at the front of the building and the 'Gold Room' to the rear, with the counter set down between the two, in what is now a passage. The designations blue and gold were taken from the respective colours of the old Lloyd loom furniture in each room. The latter were often used for naval examinations, 'runs ashore' and leaving parties. The layout of the pub (Illus 8) in those days was rather different from present-day arrangements. A corridor led from the front High St entrance all the way through to the back door, which opened out on to the courtyard at the rear. From this corridor an off-sales hatch was cut through the wall of the Long Room or public bar, popularly known as the 'Bottle and Jug'. The clientele of the usually packed 'public' were served ale in stone jug mugs with a blue rim whilst 'dixies' were the order of the day in the lounge bars when glasses ran short. The kitchen was positioned where the ladies room is now situated, the latter being sited in the garden, whilst the gents lavatories were alongside the brewery building, which flanked the north side of the rear courtyard. Another building in the courtyard was the 'Golden Lion Hut' which was hired out for weddings and other social events and only taken down in the late 1970s.

Village Pubs

The Golden Lion

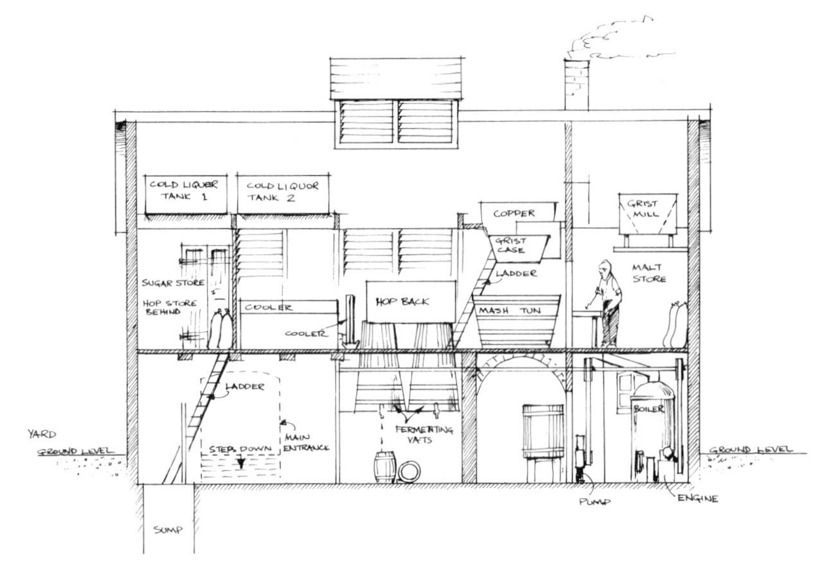

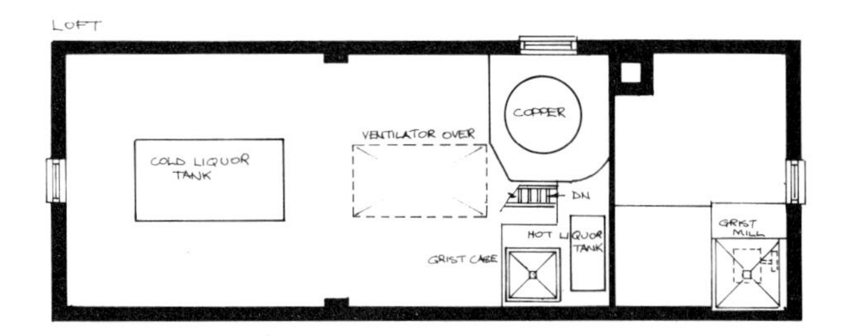

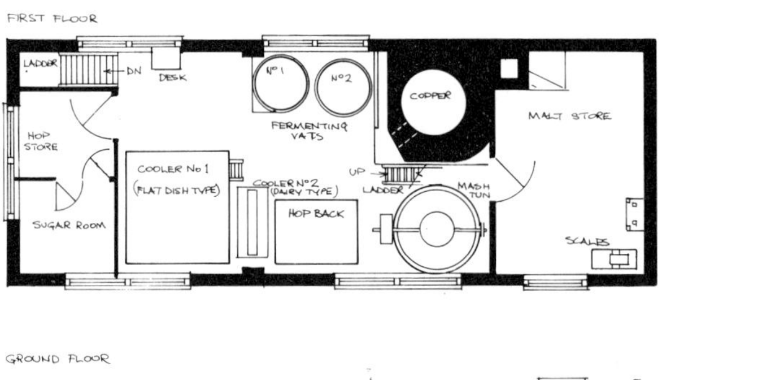

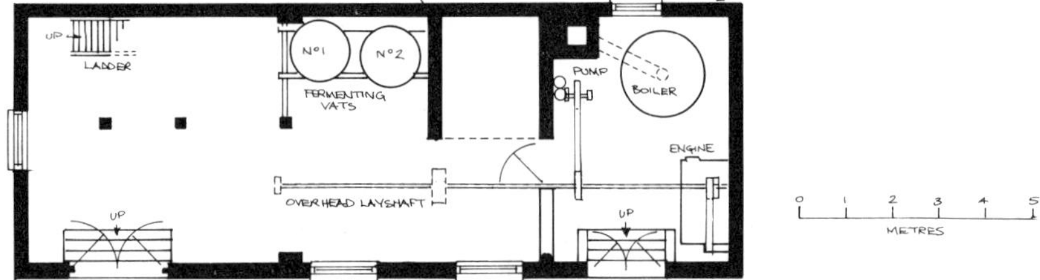

Illustration 9 The Golden Lion Brewery Layout and detail

The Brewery

Incidentally, the circular holes in the entrance doors of the Golden Lion are reputed to have been spy holes used by members of the *Oddfellows Society*. This Lodge flourished in the revolutionary years of the 1920s and 1930s and used the 'Golden' as an HQ. It was a somewhat clandestine men's club which, I have no doubt, planned to right all the wrongs (imagined or actual) suffered by the villagers at the hands of authority.

The reason for the 'Golden's' outstanding popularity was the Brewery (Illus 9) 'out the back'. Throughout the privations of the Second World War and the early postwar years, the unique nature of the pub and brewery ensured that the Golden Lion 'never ran dry'. This caused an article to be printed in the Picture Post magazine on 10th August 1946, entitled 'Pub That Brews Its Own Beer'. It extolled the virtues of a house that did not have to display signs sadly pronouncing 'no beer' or 'closed for the day'. For the younger readers it maybe necessary to point out that, during and after the Second World War, the overall shortage of essentials, and the resultant rationing, meant that most goods and foods were in short supply. Furthermore, despite the efforts of officialdom to ensure continuous and fair shares for all, there were many occasions when the shelves remained bare.

Dick Olding

Although it was not unusual for a pub to go 'hand in flagon' with a small brewery in days of yore, it is almost unique to find the original buildings and implements still wholly intact. In the case of the Golden Lion, beer was brewed as recently as 1956/1957, when the last brewmaster, Dick Olding, finally retired and his employer W J Hunt sold the business to *Courage's*. Mr Olding, 81 years old in 1957 and whose family had lived in the village for several centuries, would appear to have been the 'master of proceedings' since 1906. 'Old Dick', as he was fondly known, was well loved by one and all and (surprisingly) was a strict teetotaller. Despite this, if required, he used to help behind the bar. He was well remembered for wearing a trilby on 'best dressed days' and for 'journeying' on an old 'JAP' motorbike. Dick Olding used to produce sufficient brew for the tenants of both the Golden and Hunt's off-licence, situated in Kingston Road, Portsmouth. Between the Great Wars, two brews were made, the one known as '5s' and the other as '7s' - the beer costing 5d and the ale 7d a pint. Yes, a pint, which in modern money would be about 2p and 3p! When Dick's bad leg played up, Mr Yoxall, a Hunt's employee from Portsmouth, travelled to Southwick to give him a hand. Brothers Fred and Tom Carter, members of a well-known village family, were amongst the 'dedicated Dick Olding assistants'. Fred has unfortunately passed away but Tom still lives in the village. Apart from the Carters' appreciation of a good pint, their involvement probably owed much to their strength.

2p & 3p A Pint

Dick Olding brewing beer at the Golden Lion
PICTURE POST

A 'brewing' took place about every three months and required some six to eight 2cwt (approximately 100kg) sacks of hops to be humped up, past the first floor, to the loft and the Grist Mill. In addition, coal for the boiler had to be loaded and the spent grain removed for cattle feed. Naturally all the equipment, such as the mill, copper, casings, mash tun, tanks, coolers, fermenting vats and barrels had to be cleaned and prepared. Despite the need for the helping hand of 'muscle', 'Old Dick' oversaw the various processes by himself, taking his secrets and tricks of the trade to the grave with him. It is said, the odour was such, that anyone entering the village, with the slightest sense of smell, would realise a 'brew' was underway.

The separate brewhouse superseded an earlier one, referred to in a lease of 1898, between Thomas Thistlethwayte 'the younger' and William James Hunt, wherein the schedule details the 'old brewhouse now [a] washhouse'. In this lease, W J Hunt had to agree to use - in the brewhouse only - the best, hard, smokeless Welsh steam coal and to sell only pure beer brewed from malt and hops.

It is interesting to note that in 1860 a William Hunt was elected 'Ale Conner', a manorial appointee responsible for testing the quality of ale and beer. In 1904, when Alex Thistlethwayte was the Squire, the lease was renewed. In 1911, due to the demise of Mr Hunt, his wife Elizabeth took over the property, but the rent rose from a total of £63 (£28 for the pub and £35 for the brewery) to £72. The rise was due to the brewery being reassessed to £44.

A survey in 1970, referred to the Golden Lion brewery as being 'the most interesting in the county and that it was an excellent example of a late nineteenth century brewhouse, purpose built to supply one village public house and a certain amount of off-licence trade'* The conspicuous louvred ventilators were to disperse the heat used and developed in the process and are a feature of all old brewery buildings.

The Golden's Clients

The wartime bar staff served a lot of 'very important' people including General Eisenhower, Prince Philip and General Montgomery. It is rumoured, only rumoured, that it was Montgomery who gave one of the young barmaids the parachute cord and silk of the unexploded German land mine that had landed in the grounds of Southwick House. As previously detailed, rumour again has it that the silk was used to 'run-up' pairs of cami-knickers. With all these high-profile customers, the Golden was subject to the watchful eye of the Military Police. I suppose it was no different to the sweep of a modern-day shore patrol keeping an eye on a lively 'run ashore'.

* *With acknowledgements to an article 'A Gazetteer of Hampshire Breweries' by M F Tighe, printed in The Hampshire Field Club & Archaeological Society Proceedings, Vol 27, 1970.*

The pub's landlord.
PICTURE POST

Apart from the unavoidable intrusions into the villagers' usual way of life, imposed by the ever-increasing presence of the military machine and personnel, it is important to understand that the inhabitants of Southwick put their backs into the war effort. Moreover, this was no light-hearted approach. Forget melting down pots and pans, sacrificing iron railings, forgoing forever an old bicycle, motorbike or car. Everyone did that. Oh no, the residents of Southwick voted with their stomachs to wage war on Nazi German. They joined battle against Adolf Hitler by becoming members of 'The Hampshire County Pie Scheme' on the 4th June 1943. Never mind the proposed invasion of Europe, about which of course neither the locals nor the Germans knew anything. I am sure that if the Third Reich had realized that the noble citizenry were banding together under the banner of the 'Pie Scheme' arrangement, then their resistance would have crumbled much earlier than the resultant end to hostilities! Ho, hum! Mark you, this supreme effort was considered so devastating a weapon, that secrecy appears to have precluded any reference to this particular aspect of Southwick's war effort in the standard works of Second World War literature! There follows the substantive parts of the organisational correspondence. Readers will appreciate I am taking a risk in not hiding behind the rules governing state secrets and D Notices, but... Perhaps at this point, and in case of any doubt I must reiterate that the documents are absolutely genuine. A friend of mine, after scanning my scribblings, jotted a note in the margin of the folio 'Is this a con'?

The Pie Scheme

A Portsmouth ARP Warden exercises his right to marshall the traffic in a daylight dress rehearsal in 1940. Well, he would, wouldn't he?

THE NEWS

Others were also carrying out air raid drills in 1940,including this local Fire Brigade Unit,...

THE NEWS

...whilst yet more local lads were gathering waste-paper to help the war effort.

THE NEWS

HAMPSHIRE COUNTY PIE SCHEME

33 Southgate Street,
Winchester, Hants.

25th June, 1943.

Dear Madam,

I am enclosing a Bank Paying-in book in triplicate, which must be used every time money is paid into the Bank.

One sheet will be retained by the Bank, one must be sent to me at this office at the end of each month with your Pie Return, and the third left in the book for your own records.

Yours faithfully,

F.A.GORTON,

Secretary.

M450/5002. 10,000 pads. 12/41. 51-4043 F Memo. 2

MINISTRY OF FOOD

Memorandum

From Droxford R.D. Food Control Committee. The Institute, Bishops Waltham.

To Mrs Stagg. 15 High Street Southwick.

Ref.: VL. 5.6.43.

Pie Scheme.

Authority has been received for a Pie Scheme at Southwick commencing on June 6th with what? 300 pies weekly.

Please complete the enclosed application for a catering licence, & return the form to this office as soon as possible.

T. Pearson/VL.

Food Executive Officer.

E.L.3

Licence No. GL 23/26 333

Ministry of Food

The Defence (General) Regulations, 1939, as amended
The Food (Licensing of Establishments) Order, 1943

Pursuant to the above Order and subject to the conditions set out overleaf, the Minister of Food hereby licenses

Kate Stagg (Name of Licensee)

* Strike out whichever is inapplicable

to carry on a catering establishment* at

Southwick Pie Service, 15 High Street, Southwick. (Address of Premises)

and to obtain for the purposes of that establishment the following specified foods :—

Bacon and ham, uncooked	Fruit, bottled or canned	Milk, fresh
Bacon and ham, cooked	Fruit, crystallised	Milk, canned
Biscuits, rusks and crispbreads	Fruit, curds	Milk, dried
Blancmange powder, cornflour and custard powder	Fruit, dried or evaporated	Mincemeat
Bread	Fruit, fresh	Nuts
Butter	Game	Oatmeal and oatflakes
Cakes	Honey	Pickles and sauces
Canned beans	Jam and marmalade	Potatoes
Cereal breakfast foods	Lard and compound lard	Poultry (including turkeys)
Cheese (including processed cheese)	Macaroni, spaghetti and vermicelli	Rabbits
Cocoa	Margarine	Rice and edible rice products
Coffee	Meat, chilled, fresh or frozen	Sago and tapioca
Coffee essence (including coffee and chicory essence)	Meat, canned or preserved, other than canned corned beef, canned corned mutton and canned corned pork	Sausages
Edible and cooking fat	Meat, cooked	Semolina
Edible egg products	Meat pastes	Soups, canned or desiccated
Eggs	Meat pastries (including sausage rolls) and meat pies	Soya flour
Fish, wet	Meat products, manufactured or canned meat not in airtight containers	Sugar
Fish, cured or dried	Meat roll or galantines, canned	Syrup and treacle
Fish, in cans, glasses or other airtight containers		Table jellies
Fish pastes		Tea
Flour		Vegetables, fresh, other than potatoes
		Vegetables, bottled or canned, other than canned beans
		Vegetables, dried

Food Office Stamp: DROXFORD RURAL DISTRICT * THE INSTITUTE BISHOP'S WALTHAM * FOOD CONTROL OFFICE

Code No.

For and on behalf of the Minister of Food

T. Pearson
Food Executive Officer.

Dated the 16th day of July, 1943

P.T.O.

An air-raid could have devastating affects on both home...
THE NEWS

...and family.
THE NEWS

These rather self-conscious ARP wardens have created a 'home-from-home' in their Anderson shelter.
THE NEWS

33 Southgate Street,
Winchester,
Hants.

15th July, 1943.

Dear Madam,

Change of Address.

The Office of the Hants County Pie Scheme is being transferred from the above address to The Castle, Winchester, on the 19th of July, 1943.

Telephone: Winchester 4411, Mondays, Tuesdays, and Fridays from 10 a.m. to 4 p.m.

Yours faithfully,

F.A.Gorton,

Secretary.

Hampshire County Pie Scheme

TELEPHONE: WINCHESTER ~~2530~~

The Castle
~~33 SOUTHGATE STREET~~,
WINCHESTER

23rd July 1943

Dear Madam
Southwick & North Boarhunt

I find that you did not enclose the Bakers receipted bills when sending in the pie returns for June and I shall be glad if you will forward them as soon as Possible.
If it would not inconvenience you it would help me if you would use the paying in book numbered 108 for the parish of Southwick and the one numbered 85 for North Boarhunt as in ~~one~~ this Office each scheme goes by its number !

Yours faithfully
FAGorton
Secretary

Mrs Darlington
Oak Lodge
Southwick
near Fareham

HAMPSHIRE COUNTY PIE SCHEME.

The Castle,
Winchester.

Telephone
Winchester 4411 - Extension 8.

13th August 1943.

Dear Madam,
Up to the present the arrangement for obtaining additional pies has been for the applications to come to me but in future it has been arranged for supplementary permits to be issued by the Local Food Officer, so in future please apply to your Local Food Office.
The Ministry of Food has asked me to impress on you that you must on no account apply to your baker for pies in excess of the permits granted to you without first notifying your local Food Officer of the number of additional pies required.

Yours faithfully,

F. A. GORTON

Secretary.

In an effort to avoid the death and destruction caused by air attacks, many a community constructed sandbag shelters for the residents in their street.
THE NEWS

Mind you, the bags had to be filled. These Waterlooville youngsters appear to be enjoying the task.
THE NEWS

Butchers queuing for meat at a local distribution centre in 1940.
THE NEWS

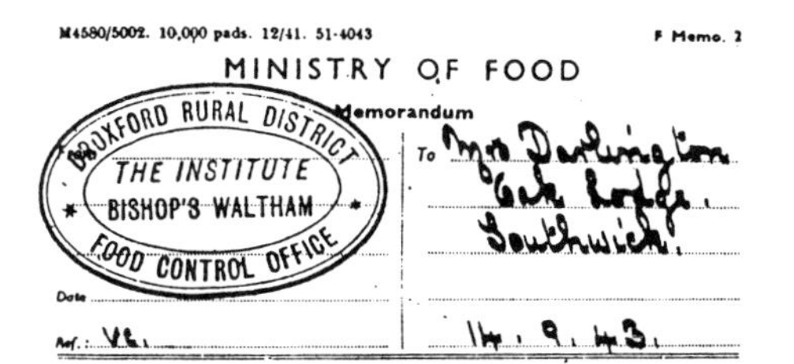
M4580/5002. 10,000 pads. 12/41. 51-4043 — F Memo. 2

MINISTRY OF FOOD

Memorandum

DROXFORD RURAL DISTRICT — THE INSTITUTE — BISHOP'S WALTHAM — FOOD CONTROL OFFICE

To Mrs Darlington, Oak Lodge, Southwick.

Date 14.9.43.

Ref.: VL.

Dear Madam.

Please complete the enclosed E.G.C.3a to show the number of pies distributed from your centre each week during the eight weeks ending September 18th 1943.

The week numbers are 1 to 8 and the pies should be entered in the column headed subs. meals.

No other entry need be made, except to sign the form before returning it.

Yours faithfully.

F. Pearson

Food Executive Officer.

HAMPSHIRE COUNTY PIE SCHEME.

Telephone.
Winchester 4411,
Extension 8.

THE CASTLE,
WINCHESTER.

17th December 1943.

Dear Madam,

Monthly Returns.

The periods of the monthly returns are to be altered to comprise the whole of each calendar month instead of the four weekly periods and this will mean that four times a year there will be five weeks in one period.

The change will take place in the New Year and in order to clear up the odd weeks in December, I shall be glad if you will, within the first ten days of January, send me in a return to include these weeks and then afterwards send in a return at the end of each calendar month.

I enclose a few return forms in case you need them, but the old forms can still be used by altering "four weeks ending______" to the "month of_______".

In the cases where the baker is not paid weekly, I am asking the bakers in future to make their bills out for each calendar month to co-incide with your monthly returns.

Yours faithfully,

F. A. GORTON,

Secretary.

DROXFORD RURAL DISTRICT — S33 — FOOD OFFICE

MINISTRY OF FOOD. F323A.

To:

Name and Address of Mrs Darlington

Establishment Pie Services,

Southwick & North Boarhunt.

20.1.44

Dear ~~Sir~~/Madam,

Your return on Form E.G.C.3 for the eight weeks ended Jan 8/44 which was due in this office on Jan 15/44 has not yet been received.

The statistics compiled from these returns are of the utmost importance to the work of the Ministry of Food and it is essential therefore that establishments should render them promptly. I should be obliged accordingly if you would send the above return to this office immediately and ensure that future returns are made by not later than the due date.

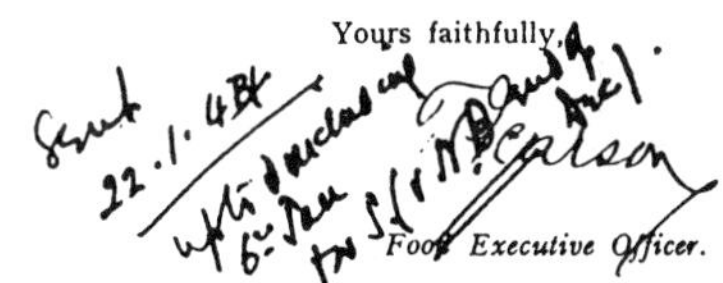
Yours faithfully,

F. Pearson

Food Executive Officer.

Par. 41 (5) G344 5M/4/43 (2) G393 5M/6/43 (2)

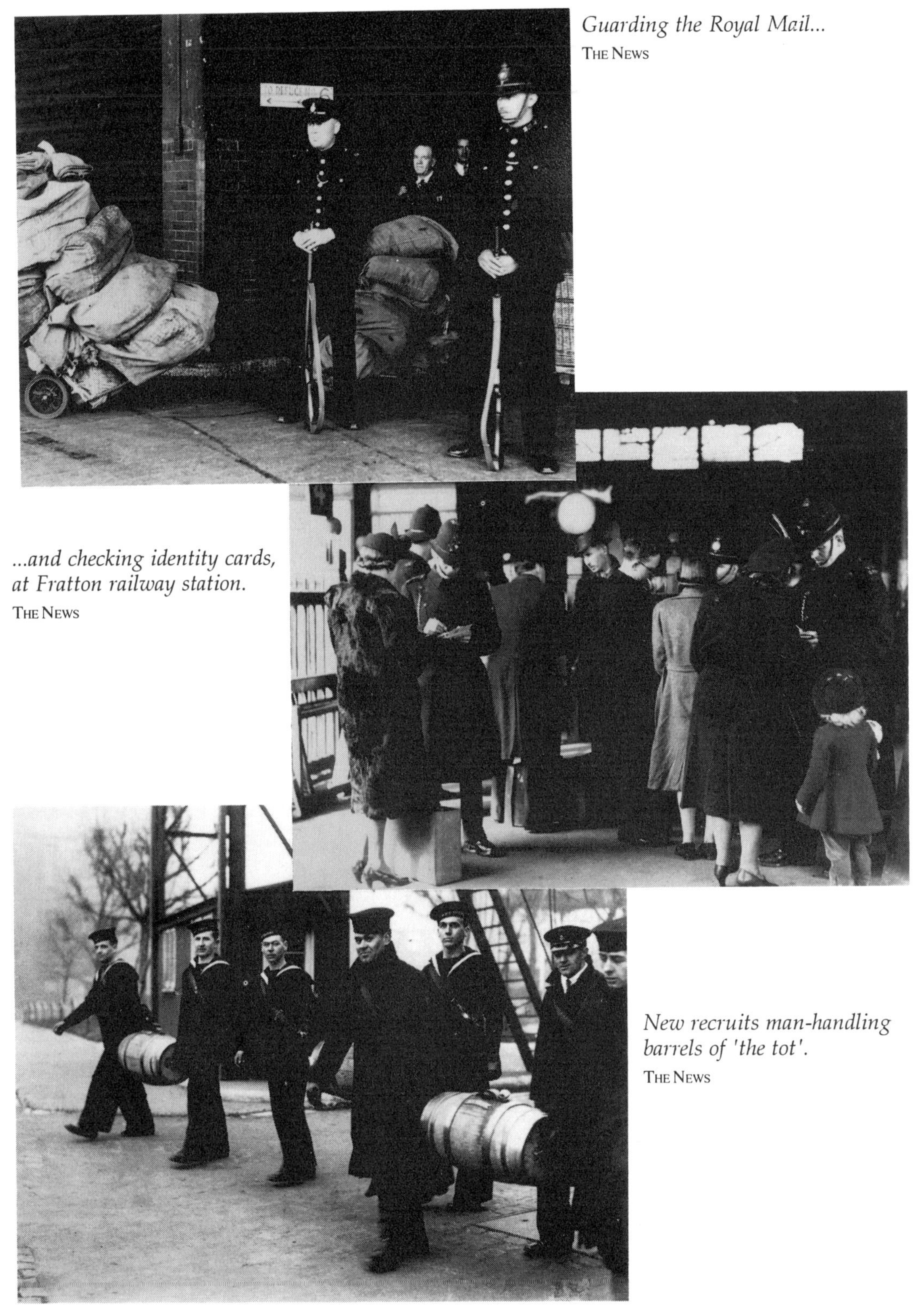

Guarding the Royal Mail...
THE NEWS

...and checking identity cards, at Fratton railway station.
THE NEWS

New recruits man-handling barrels of 'the tot'.
THE NEWS

Hampshire County Pie Scheme

TELEPHONE:
WINCHESTER 4411, EXT. 8.

THE CASTLE,
WINCHESTER.

24th January 1944

Dear Madam,

Southwick & North Boarhunt

Thank you for sending in your Pie returns for December with the receipted baker's bills.

I notice that the return for Southwick is for the 14th and 16th of December, I presume this is correct and that no pies were delivered in December after this date ?

Yours faithfully

[signature]
Secretary

Mrs Darlington,
Oak Lodge,
Southwick
near Fareham

ans. 1/2/44

(85168) 51508 3/43 745/16 F Memo. 2

MINISTRY OF FOOD

Memorandum

DROXFORD RURAL DISTRICT
THE INSTITUTE
BISHOP'S WALTHAM
FOOD CONTROL OFFICE

To Mrs Darlington,
Oak Lodge,
Southwick.

Date 27th January 1944

Ref.: VC

Dear Madam.

Meat Pie Schemes
Southwick & North Boarhunt.

Your EGC 3 shows that you are distributing considerably less pies than your authorities for these schemes allow. I shall be glad if you will let me know if the distribution during the last eight weeks can be taken as representing your present requirements.

Please sign the EGC 3's and return them to this office as early as possible.

Yours faithfully.

T. Pearson

Food Executive Officer.

ans. 31.1.44 P.T.O.

To. The Food Executive Officer

Dear Sir. I duly return my E.G.C 3 sh: I have signed herewith.
I regret to say that I think Southwick is not as keen on having the pies as they were & I have noted a steady decline in numbers.
On the other hand we purposely refrained fr ordering Pies over Christmas, by special request, as we understood this was in accordance with the rest of the district who were desirous of giving the bakers a rest.

Yrs faithfully
T Darlington
31.1.44

The Home Guard was formed to defy the expected German invasion and to maintain internal law and order. Whether they would have caused more than a blip in the advance of enemy front-line troops is debatable. On the other hand, the affection in which they were held can be judged by their soubriquet - 'Dad's Army'.
THE NEWS

The Cosham branch,...
THE NEWS

...the Wickham boys...
THE NEWS

...and those of Havant.
THE NEWS

(85168) 51508 3/43 745/16 F Memo. 2

MINISTRY OF FOOD

Memorandum

DROXFORD RURAL DISTRICT
THE INSTITUTE
BISHOP'S WALTHAM
FOOD CONTROL OFFICE

To Mrs Darlington,
Oak Lodge,
Southwick.

Date

Ref.: VC

2nd February 1944

Dear Madam.

The authorities for pies from Messrs Cases Bakery Ltd, Wickham have been revised and are now as follows:-
Southwick 228
North Boarhunt 96 pies weekly.

Yours faithfully.

T. Pearson

Food Executive Officer.

Hampshire County Pie Scheme

TELEPHONE:
WINCHESTER 4411, EXT. 8.

THE CASTLE,
WINCHESTER.
21st February 1944

Dear Madam,

North Boarhunt

Thank you for sending in the returns for North Boarhumt and Southwick.

It will be quite in order for you to pay in the missing 6D when you pay in the money for February.

I have made a note to the effect that Southwick is only having pies on Fridays in future.

Yours faithfully

Secretary

Mrs Darlington
Oak Lodge
Southwick
Fareham
Hants

In the meantime, a Colonel Sloane-Stanley inspects the Gosport lads,...

(I bet he was a tyro in the Boer War).

THE NEWS

...whilst the Wickham Home Guard is trusted with an automatic weapon, instead of broomsticks and pitchforks,...

THE NEWS

...and these 'worthies' take a tea-break from exercises on Butser Hill.

THE NEWS

5 Widley Lane
Purbrook
Portsmouth
Hants.
March 10. 1944.

Dear Madam.

I have written to the Food Officer at Droxford about the meat pies they told me to apply to you about them. Do I have to get a permit for them. Would you let me know if they deliver them or do we have to come & fetch them. Living such a long way from Southwick I should not be able to come for them.

Yours Faithfully

A. Singleton

15/3/44

Hampshire County Pie Scheme

THE CASTLE
~~33 SOUTHGATE STREET~~,
WINCHESTER

TELEPHONE:
WINCHESTER ~~[illegible]~~
4411 Ext:8

14th April 1944

Dear Mrs Darlington
North Boarhunt & Southwick

Thank you for your letter and pie returns for March.
I note that you have paid in 1/- too much for North Boarhunt, please deduct this amount when you next pay in money to the pie account for this place and it will be quite alright.

Yours sincerely

[signature]
Secretary

Mrs A.J.Darlington
Oak Lodge
Southwick
near. Fareham
Hants

This Heinkel did not make it home, being shot down by RAF 'fighters' close by Denmead. It is said that a local landlord and a helper captured the enemy crew with a toy pistol and a 2/- coin!
THE NEWS

A crashed enemy bomber that merited attention of two local nurses,...
THE NEWS

...whilst this protagonist received a masculine guard.
THE NEWS

Hampshire County Pie Scheme

TELEPHONE:
WINCHESTER ~~2309 AND 2300~~
4411 Ext: 8.

THE CASTLE
~~33 SOUTHGATE STREET,~~
WINCHESTER

15th May 1944

Dear Mrs Darlington
SOUTHWICK.

Thank you for sending in your pie returns for North Boarhunt and Southwick.

I find that you have entered 1/- as Petty cash for Southwick and instead of deducting it from the ½d levy of £1.5.6 you have added it on and paid in £1.6.6., which of course is 2/- too much and there is also the 1/- paid in excess last month for North Boarhunt so that altogether you appear to have paid in 3/- too much, perhaps you will be good enough to adjust this when next you pay money into the Pie Account.

Yours sincerely

F A Gorton.
Secretary

Mrs Darlington
Oak Lodge
Southwick
near Fareham.

HAMPSHIRE COUNTY PIE SCHEME.

The Castle,
Winchester.

Telephone:
Winchester 4411, Ext. 8.

19th June 1944.

Dear Madam,

I beg to inform you that the County Pie Committee have decided to reduce the price of the meat pies to the public from 4d to 3½d and in future to pay all expenses incurred in running the scheme throughout the County out of the profits accumulated since the commencement of the Pie Scheme.

The alteration in the price will take place on the 2nd July, therefore after this date all pies should be sold at 3½d each.

It will still be necessary for you to send in a return at the end of each calendar month with the receipted bakers bills.

Any expenses incurred in running your scheme will in future be paid from this Office, either on receipt of your monthly return or in the case of small amounts under 10/-, every three months.

Please enter the details of any petty cash expenditure clearly on the monthly return, sending receipts wherever possible.

I enclose a few monthly returns.

Yours faithfully,

F. A. GORTON,

Secretary.

Some ladies joined the Women's Land Army and ploughed up the downs,...
THE NEWS

...others practised home fire drills (with a stirrup pump),...
THE NEWS

...some became volunteer ambulance drivers, as did these women at Fareham,...
THE NEWS

(Surely this is a Lanchester?)

...and yet others drove Emergency Food Vans.
THE NEWS

MINISTRY OF FOOD

Telegrams "Foodtender"

Telephone: Bishops Waltham 203

Your ref.........

M.O.F. ref. VC

NATIONAL REGISTRATION
RURAL DISTRICT OF DROXFORD

S 33 EEF

THE INSTITUTE
BANK STREET
BISHOP'S WALTHAM
SOUTHAMPTON

7th August 1945.

Dear Madam.

I have not yet received your E.G.C.3 for the Pie Centres at Southwick and North Boarhunt. These returns were due at this office on July 29th. Please forward by return.

Yours faithfully.

T. Pearson

Food Executive Officer.

Mrs Darlington,
Oak Lodge,
Southwick.

Hampshire County Pie Scheme

TELEPHONE: WINCHESTER 4411, EXT. 8.

THE CASTLE,
WINCHESTER.

24th August 1945

Dear Mrs Darlington,
Southwick & North Boarhunt

Thank you for sending in your pie returns for the month of July.
I agree with you that after the end of September the scheme might be given up, unless there is more demand for the pies.
Are the people who have the pies, poor people who really want them do you know?

Yours sincerely

Secretary

Mrs Darlington
Oak Lodge
Southwick
near Fareham

Hampshire County Pie Scheme

TELEPHONE: WINCHESTER 4411, EXT. 8.

THE CASTLE,
WINCHESTER.

28th August 1944

Dear Madam,
North Boarhunt & Southwick

I have received your letter of the 20th inst, and think it will be best to carry on with the pies for the present as I see you still sell quite a few pies, and I think they do fill a want especially in the winter when there are not so many vegetables about.
If at any time the number of pies drop to two or three dozen, I think we might consider stopping the scheme.

Yours faithfully

Secretary

Mrs Darlington
Oak Lodge
Southwick
near Fareham.

The Nation engaged in an orgy of assembling and collecting salvage for recycling and melting down as machines and weapons of war. Here Portchester Boy Scouts collect waste paper to swell the funds to purchase an ambulance,...
THE NEWS

...these ladies pile up old pots and pans,...
THE NEWS

...and these gentlemen take a last ride on a car chassis at a Fareham yard.
THE NEWS

Before you complete this form, read carefully the instructions overleaf. E.G.C.3

DECLARATION

I hereby declare that to the best of my knowledge and belief the particulars given by me on this form are correct, and that the stocks declared have been ascertained by physical stock-taking at the close of the 8-week period ended on 5th Jan 1946.

Establishment: Pie Centre, Southwick.

Licence No. EL 23/26. Estab. group A23.

Signature: Mrs S. J. Buckley

Position in establishment: in charge of pie scheme for Southwick

Date: Jan 26 – 1946

Coupons collected: TEA (total No. of weekly coupons) | POINTS (total points value)

Do not complete this column unless instructed to do so: a, b

RESIDENTS (enter No. separately for each week and add all together on line 6)

RETURN OF HOT BEVERAGES AND MEALS SERVED AS COMPILED FROM DAILY RECORD (Institutions: enter only the hot beverages and meals served to non-residents)

HOT BEVS.	WEEK No.	PIES	BREAKFASTS	SUBS. MEALS	TEA MEALS
	17	7 dozen			
	18	7 dozen			
	19	4½ dozen			
	20	6½ dozen			
	21	6 dozen			
	22	4 dozen			
	23	none			
	24	6 dozen			

6 Enter on this line the totals for the 8-weeks and copy on line 7 below: a + b | 0 R/W | 1 HB | 2 All meals (cols. 3-6) M | 3 40½ doz. MM | 4 B | 5 S | 6 T

7 Copy on this line the 8-week totals appearing on line 6 above. Keep this line clear unless otherwise instructed		RES./WKS.	HOT BEVS.	ALL MEALS	MAIN MEALS	BREAKFASTS	SUBS. MEALS	TEA MEALS
					40½ doz pies			

E.G.C.3A

INSTRUCTIONS (continued, for completing this side of form):

4. On the E.G.C.3 part above, enter under "coupons collected" the total number of weekly tea coupons and the total points value of the points taken from residents' ration books during the 8-week period.
5. Under "Return of hot beverages, etc.," in the column with the heavy lines headed "WEEK No." fill in the ration week numbers; for each week enter the number of residents, of hot beverages, and of each type of meal served as defined overleaf. INSTITUTIONS must not on any account include hot beverages or meals served to residents.
6. Add the entries for the 8 weeks and enter the totals on line 6; add the totals so entered in columns marked 3, 4, 5 and 6, and write the answer in column marked 2; copy on line 7 all totals appearing on line 6.
7. Complete and sign the above declaration (the signature must be that of the proprietor, manager or some other responsible person), and send this form to the Food Office together with the tea and points coupons collected.

M.25192/4776 4/45 750M Ho. (370)

Food Office stamp: URBAN DISTRICT S33 FOOD OFFICE

Copy of return by catering establishments and institutions for the 8-week period ended on 5th Jan 1946.

Establishment: Pie Centre, Southwick.

Licence No. EL 23/26. Estab. group A23.

(copy of line 4) Quantities 5 Obtained during the 8-week period	TEA cwts. lbs.	PRESERVES cwts. lbs. (other than marmalade) (marmalade)	FATS cwts. lbs. (c, f, b, m)	SUGAR cwts. lbs.	CHEESE cwts. lbs.	Copy of line 4 totals for the whole 8-week period	MEAT £ s.	BACON cwts. lbs.	FISH cwts. lbs. (filleted) (unfilleted)

CONDITIONS

1. This licence does not entitle the holder to carry on an establishment except at the premises specified hereon, or to obtain specified foods for the purposes of an establishment except that carried on at the said premises.

NOTES

1. This licence incorporates the conditions set out in the Second Schedule to the above Order.
2. This licence is not transferable and may be revoked at any time.
3. Infringements of the conditions of this licence are offences against the Defence (General) Regulations, 1939.
4. In the event of the establishment carried on at the above address being closed down, the holder of this licence or his authorised agent shall return the licence to the Food Executive Officer by whom it has been issued.

Even Church bells were silenced,...
THE NEWS

These items collected by a Gosport ARP Warden might well finish up...
THE NEWS

...on a pile like this.
THE NEWS

MINISTRY OF FOOD

EGC3/EGC3A

(8-WEEKLY RETURN BY CATERING ESTABLISHMENTS AND INSTITUTIONS)

NOTICE

This form must be completed in accordance with the instructions set out below and returned to the Food Office, whose stamp appears overleaf, within 7 days from the end of the 8-week period to which the form relates.

The information is required for the purpose of Orders made under the Defence (General) Regulations, 1939, and any false statement will be an offence against those Regulations.

INSTRUCTIONS

1. No entry asked for may be left blank; either fill it in or enter "nil"; on no account enter anything not asked for.
2. Complete as follows the E.G.C.3 part appearing on this side below the line of perforation:—
   (a) In columns tea to cheese enter in cwts. and lbs. (ignore ozs.) STOCK on line 1, quantities OBTAINED on line 4. Note in regard to FATS that "cf" cooking fat, "b" butter, "m" margarine, may be entered EITHER singly OR all three combined into one figure.
   (b) Alongside the meat column enter the ration week numbers; for each week enter the quantities obtained—of meat stated in £ and s. (ignore pence), of bacon stated in cwts. and lbs. (ignore ozs.); add the entries for the 8 weeks and enter the total of each column on line 4.
   (c) In fish column enter in cwts. and lbs. (ignore ozs.) the quantities obtained for each 4-week period, and on line 4 the total for the two periods together, giving in every case the "filleted" separately from the "unfilleted."
3. Fold the form so that the instructions you are reading are turned back and only the E.G.C.3 part below the line of perforation is left facing you. When you do this you will find line 5 immediately below line 4. Copy on this line 5 all totals appearing on line 4. Then unfold the form so that the other side faces you, and proceed in accordance with the instructions you will find there. In proceeding, be guided by the following definitions.

Definitions

(a) "RESIDENTS" mean persons whose coupons have to be cancelled or detached in any week. Note, coupons must be cancelled or detached in the following cases:—
   i. After a person (including the resident proprietor or manager, or any member of his family, and any resident staff) has spent 5 consecutive nights in an establishment, and at the end of every further period of 7 consecutive nights during which the person remains in the establishment.
   ii. In the case of all employees in an establishment who do not reside on the premises but who are provided with all or substantially all their meals on 5 or more days a week.

(b) "HOT BEVERAGE" means a hot beverage in which added sugar is customarily consumed, whether served alone or with a meal; it does not mean any spirituous beverage.

(c) "MAIN MEAL" means a meal except breakfast at which is served a course containing a portion of meat, fish, poultry, game or eggs, or a correspondingly substantial dish which is accompanied by—
   i. a helping of potatoes or other vegetables (including salads); or
   ii. one or two other courses.

(d) "BREAKFAST" means a substantial meal served during the normal breakfast period—for example, a meal including porridge, breakfast cereal, fish, bacon, egg or sausage. A meal which includes only bread, toast, butter, margarine or preserves is a tea meal not a breakfast.

(e) "SUBSIDIARY MEAL" means:
   i. a meal consisting of sandwiches, meat pies or other snacks, unaccompanied by other courses; or
   ii. any other meal except breakfast which is more substantial than a tea meal but does not contain any course which would make it a main meal.

(f) "TEA MEAL" means a meal at which only articles such as ices, bread, rolls, toast, scones, buns, butter, margarine, preserves, cakes or biscuits are served, whether or not accompanied by tea or other beverage (hot or cold).

		TEA cwts.	TEA lbs.	PRESERVES (other than marmalade) cwts.	PRESERVES lbs.	FATS cwts.	FATS lbs.	SUGAR cwts.	SUGAR lbs.	CHEESE cwts.	CHEESE lbs.
1 Stock at the end of the 8-week period.				(marmalade) cwts. lbs.		c f / b / m					
2 →	A + Sn										
Keep this shaded portion clear for use of food office											
3 →	O + So										
4 Quantities Obtained during the 8-week period.				(other than marmalade) / (marmalade)		c f / b / m					

MINISTRY OF FOOD

EGC.3

Other Quantities **Obtained**

WEEK No.	MEAT (Rationed only) at maximum retail prices £	MEAT s.	BACON CAT. "A" cwts.	BACON lbs.	FISH cwts.	FISH lbs.
					1st 4-weeks (filleted)	
					(unfilleted)	
					2nd 4-weeks (filleted)	
					(unfilleted)	
Totals for the whole 8-week period					(filleted)	
					(unfilleted)	

Takings Date	P.A. £ s. d	Persons	Value £ s. d	Payments W.V.S. [illegible]	Case. [illegible]
June					
10	1.7.8.	84	1. 8.0	3. 6.	84 1.4.6
15.	1.6.4	144	2.8.0.	6.0	144 2.2.0.
17.	7.8	117. PA canals 3	1.19.0 1.0.	4.10½ 1½	129 1.15.0
22	2.8	142 PA canals 1	2.7.4 4	5.11.½	144 2.2.0
24	.8.	121.	2.0.4	10.4½ 5.0½	123 1.15.10½
29.	—	150	2.10.0	6.3.	150 2.3.9
July 1. 3.9.8	4.8	135	2.5.0.	1.17.3. 5.7½	132 1.18.6. for [illegible] + 1/-

It was difficult to travel the lanes in and around Southwick village without bumping into khaki-clad men charging about.
THE NEWS

The vehicle occupant appears bemused rather than terrified by the sight of our men charging the thoroughfare!
THE NEWS

Here 'our lads' the stream that flows across Pigeonhouse Lane. The soldier at the rear of the first column seems reluctant to get his trouser bottoms wet!
THE NEWS

Perhaps they had spotted a low-flying brace of pheasants. I'm sure Col Thistlethwayte would have remonstrated if that had been so.
THE NEWS

CHAPTER 4

THE VILLAGE BATTLES ON

1943-1944

OVERLORD

It will be recalled (Chapter 3) that at the Casablanca Conference, early in 1943, the Summer of 1944 had been chosen for the invasion of Northern France. This operation was to be code-named OVERLORD. Previous incursions on to German held coastline, such as those at at Anzio, Dieppe and Salerno, had proved disastrous. Thus, the Allied Commanders accepted that the new plan must be foolproof, with as little room for foul-ups as was humanly possible. This laudable objective was that much more difficult to achieve as the operation had, not only to encompass an armada of craft sufficient to ship an enormous number of soldiers and armoury, but the force would have to 'enjoy' the benefit of an unbreakable air and sea support. No small task. The main objectives set down were never 'even momentarily abandoned', as proudly reported by Dwight Eisenhower, in his book *Crusade In Europe*, published in 1948 by William Heinemann. They were to:-

Eisenhower's Objectives

a. Land on the Normandy coast.
b. Build up the resources needed for a decisive battle in the Normandy-Brittany region and break out of the enemy's encircling positions. (Land operations in the first two phases were to be under the tactical direction of General Montgomery.)
c. Pursue on a broad front with two army groups, emphasizing the left to gain necessary ports and reach the boundaries of Germany and threaten the Ruhr. On the right to link up with the forces that were to invade France from the south.
d. Build up a new base along the western border of Germany, by securing ports in Belgium and in Brittany as well as in the Mediterranean.
e. While building up the forces for the final battles, keep up an unrelenting offensive to ... both to wear down the enemy and to gain advantages for the final fighting.
f. Complete the destruction of enemy forces west of the Rhine, in the meantime constantly seeking bridgeheads across the river.
g. Launch the final attack as a double envelopment of the Rhur, again emphasising the left, and follow this up by an immediate thrust through Germany, with the specific direction to be determined at the time.
h. Clean out the remainder of Germany.'

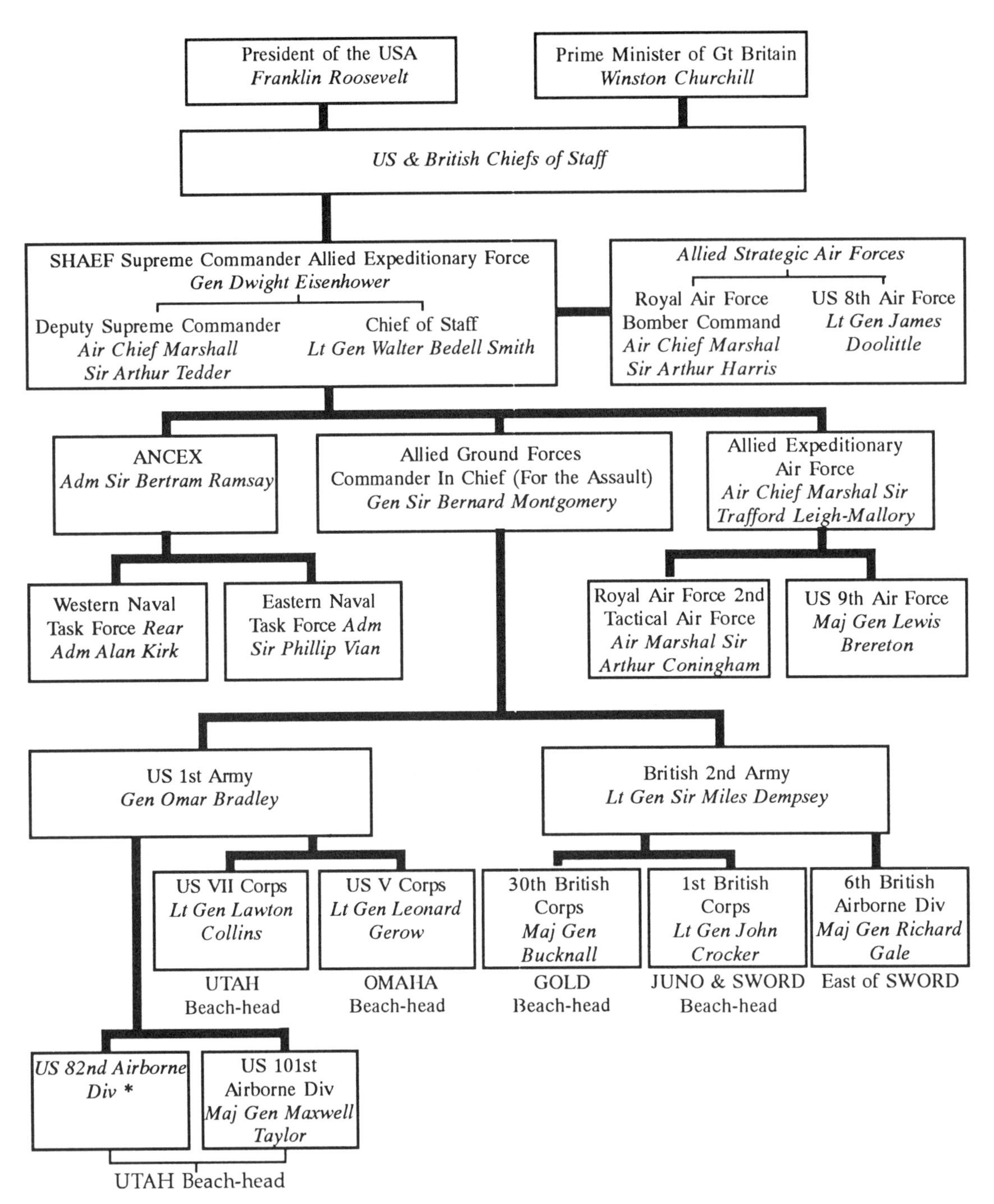

* Either Maj Gen Matthew Ridgeway or Brig Gen James Gavin, there is confusion!
Eisenhower in his book *Crusade in Europe*, published by Heinemann, lists Gavin with Rideway as Commander of the 18th US Airborne Corps, whilst others have Ridgeway as the Division Commander

Illustration 10 The Overall Command Structure, immediately prior to D-Day

The Command Structure

At a further conference held in Cairo, in November 1943, Roosevelt and Churchill thrashed out the tricky question of the command structure (Illus 10) to put Operation OVERLORD into effect. Tricky? The fact of the matter was that the Americans were supplying the bulk of the men, machines and money - the UK the 'real estate', with a powerful naval presence and an acceptable air force. The Headquarters organization, initialled SHAEF (Supreme Headquarters Allied Expeditionary Forces), was initially to be based at Bushey Park, Hertfordshire. The chosen Supreme Allied Commander was an American, one General Dwight D Eisenhower. The Deputy Supreme Commander was Air Chief Marshal Sir Arthur Tedder and Lieutenant General Walter Bedell Smith was Eisenhower's Chief of Staff. Immediately answerable to the Supreme Allied Commander were two Army groups. The American one was to be under the command of General Omar Bradley. The British and Dominion forces were to be in the 'care of' General Bernard L Montgomery, Land Forces Commander 21st Army Group, established at St Paul's School, Nr Hammersmith, London. In fact, Montgomery was to command all the army troops during and after the landings, until there was a sufficient front to allow the two army groups to operate independently of each other.

SHAEF

The Supreme Allied Commander

Gen. Bradley
'Monty'

It may have been chance but 'Monty' had been educated at St Paul's. Even more of a coincidence is that I am also an 'Old Pauline' and whiled away many a wet afternoon in the 1950s as a student idly studying the war plan map in the vaulted school lecture room. The Allied Naval Commander (of the) Expeditionary Forces (ANCXF) was Admiral Bertram Ramsay, with an HQ at Norfolk House, St James Sq, London. Air Chief Marshal Trafford Leigh-Mallory was Allied Air Commander, established at Stanmore, Middlesex. Various Army Groups and the Tactical Air HQ were sited at Uxbridge, Middlesex.

ANCXF & Admiral Ramsay

Air Marshal Leigh-Mallory

The St Paul's School Conference

The first combined conference held to introduce everyone and tactically indoctrinate the team was held in the lecture room at St Paul's School on the 7th April. A further grand presentation was made on the 15th May, in the same setting, but to an audience which not only included almost every military big-wig in uniform, but also Prime Minister Winston Churchill and King George VI.

The Teheran Conference & OVERLORD Delayed

Immediately prior to the previously referred to Cairo meeting, the three major Allies, America, Gt Britain and Russia, had met at Teheran, Iran. There General Joseph Stalin had been assured that OVERLORD would take place no later than the 1st May. Despite these promises, on the 1st February 1944 the fateful day had to be put back to the 1st June - or thereabouts. This was due to the necessity to build even more landing-craft, to enable the forces to be transported across the Channel. There's a good reason! (Although out-

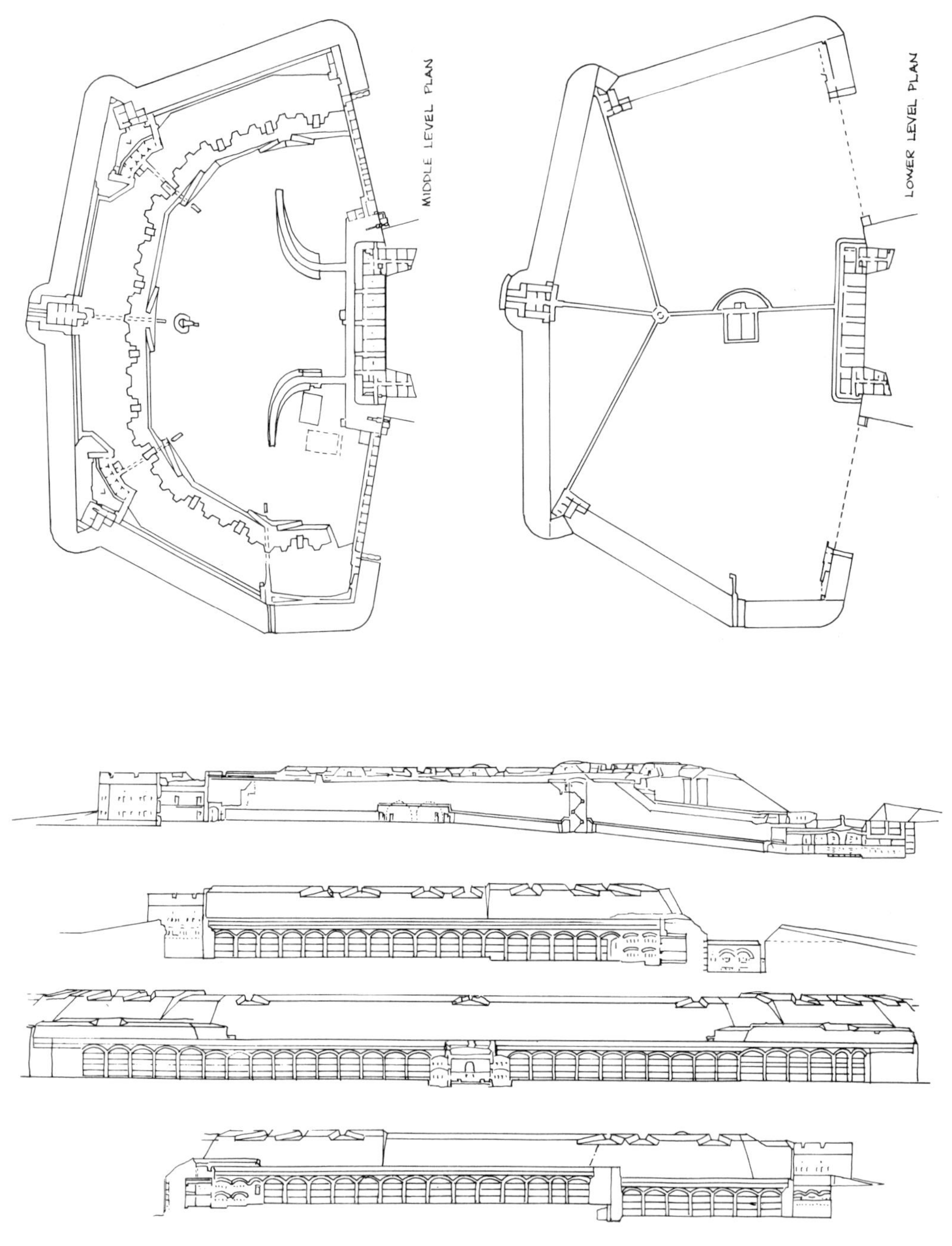

Illustration 11 Fort Southwick
Almost unbelievably, the Victorian Forts were still regarded as secret constructions. Thus, no map or chart, up to the Second World War, detailed their positions.

side the scope of this book, it is thought-provoking that much of the reason for the shortage of the desperately required landing craft and troop assault vessels could be laid at the executive door of an American Admiral who was not at all impressed by all this European invasion idea! Unfortunately he was in charge of what went where.)

Once Operation OVERLORD was well advanced and the day of launching the massive offensive loomed large, it became necessary to consider a location at which to concentrate the various command structures 'under one roof'. Ideally, this had to be close to the epicentre of the huge armada of ships being gathered together for loading with men and equipment. The chosen waters were the Solent, the main focal points radiating out from the various ports and harbours of Portsmouth Harbour and Southampton Water. With hindsight, it is easy to understand why the search for an HQ narrowed down and concentrated on Southwick Estate and the surrounding area. Strange to relate, the final selection of the D-Day HQ was greatly influenced by the earlier choice of Fort Southwick as the location from which the invasion fleet was to be monitored, the coordination centre for the landings, once the fateful 'nod' had been given. This latter decision had already been made and, as with much else to do with Southwick over the centuries, was yet another of a continuing string of extraordinary coincidences. That control centre was to be Fort Southwick, built about 1861, on land purchased from Southwick's then Lord of the Manor, Thomas Thistlethwayte. This fort was one of a number of like structures spaced along the brow of the hill overlooking the approaches to Portsmouth Harbour. They were constructed in order to guard against the threat of a French invasion, considered in the 19th century to be a distinct possibility.

Fort Southwick

Initially, Fort Southwick was appropriated as the headquarters for Admiral Sir Charles Little, Commander in Chief, Portsmouth Command, in 1942. To make that move possible, a new military road was laid down as early as January 1941. A newspaper photograph of the period shows the Hampshire War Agricultural Committee ploughing Portsdown Hill 'to cultivate a barley crop'. This 'top of the slope' thoroughfare was not opened to the public until many years after the end of hostilities - and then only after a cam paign of 'driver disobedience'. A number of alterations (Illus 11) to the fort were necessary in order to create a bombproof, comprehensive Naval Operation Control Centre with associated communications capability. The underground workings were excavated by Welsh and Belgian miners of the Pioneer Corps, who were quartered in the upper fort. The operation tunnels were about 100ft and 150 steps beneath the surface. The layout comprised three steel and brick lined main tunnels running parallel to each other and linked by twelve cross passages, which provided office space, some galley facilities

A member of the 'Hants War Agricultural Committee' (the what?) ploughing the top of Portsdown Hill for a barley crop in January 1941. Note the new road being forged through to Fort Southwick. And where is the roundabout?

THE NEWS

It is reported that these 3.7 inch guns, bolted down on Fort Southwick and which 'threw forth' a 28lb shell, were able to fire at some ten rounds a minute.

THE NEWS

as well as cabin and dormitory accommodation. In addition, two other tunnels and one cross passage were utilised as gangways and for emergency, off-watch bunk sleeping. Air conditioning was installed as well as fresh water storage.

The Fort is selected As UGHQ

But the utilisation of Fort Southwick as the Combined Underground Operations Headquarters (or UGHQ) for Operation OVERLORD in 1944 ensured that the old, mouldering Victorian fortification seized a permanent place in the 'spotlight of military history'. This may have been the second role in its history (or third, depending how you number) but without doubt it was the most important. Fort Southwick, situated on top of Portsdown Hill and overlooking the Solent, could almost have been built all those years ago, just for this victorious event. From the maze of tunnels beneath the 19thC fortification the D-Day naval operations were controlled. It would be an understatement to record that its location was a closely guarded secret. Located deep within the burrowed out chalk were the teleprinters, switchboards and coding operations through which all the incoming and outgoing signal traffic passed. At the centre of a vast network of underground tunnel-shaped, air-conditioned offices, where Navy, Army and Air Force staff were to work together, was the all important Naval Plotting Room. From this emerged a complete picture of the pivotal naval participation in the invasion, information that was continuously available to the Allied Commanders. If the atmosphere needed any further intensification, the stress was heightened because the up-to-then-secret, newly developed system of radio telegraphy techniques had to be tried out - prior to 'battlefield' action. Fortunately, everything worked well.

Accommodation Problems At The Fort

In 1944, accommodation at the fort was a severe problem due to the large influx of WRNS! Many had to be quartered in caravans and tents sited in the building's original moat. In addition, there was a battery of anti-aircraft crew to be billeted and they had to use the tunnels as living quarters.

To understand the importance of the role the Fort and staff played in the grand scheme of things, it is only necessary to record Admiral Ramsey's signal, sent soon after the D-Day landings, which read:

> 'The main burden of the operation on the naval side was perforce borne by the Portsmouth Command.'

The planned invasion of occupied Northern Europe by the Allied Forces was the most ambitious, if not the greatest amphibious operation ever to be mounted in the history of war - a task controlled from the UGHQ Fort Southwick. The immense scale of the planned event can be appreciated if it is noted that the proposed fleet comprised:

As the preparations and momentum of Operation OVERLORD gathered pace, so did the activities of service men and women. Inevitably, soldiers marched!
THE IWM H442200

Other men scaled and abseiled up and down the face of Portsdown Hill...
THE NEWS

...and War Correspondents sat down for a 'fireside chat' by Major Gen F W de Guingand in Southwick School. The Major General was the 21st Army Group Chief of Staff.
THE IWM H39473

7 Battleships, 23 Cruisers, 93 Destroyers, 71 Corvettes, 63 Frigates and Destroyer Escorts. And these were in addition to a vast assembly of assault, troop and tank landing craft accompanied by numbers of liners and passenger ships converted to use as troop carriers and hospital ships - a total of between 7,000 & 9,000 boats.

The Composition of the Fleet

A Wren's Tale

A wartime 'Wren' based at Fort Southwick during the build-up to D-Day recalls*:

'I was working as a personal secretary before the War. After the Munich crisis, I volunteered to join the WRNS. Due to a shortage of switchboard operators, I became one after training at the Dockyard, Portsmouth.
As a result of bomb-damage to the Dockyard telegraphic exchange and offices of the Commander-in-Chief we were moved to Fort Wallington, Portsdown Hill. Whilst there, I learnt that a new Communications Centre and Commander-in-Chief's Headquarters was being prepared at Fort Southwick - just along the road. The subject was surrounded with great secrecy, but I was delighted when my Signals Officer asked me to accompany him to look over the new 'exchange', where at a later date I took charge of over 100 telephone operators.
Security at Fort Southwick was intense and armed sentries challenged us as we approached the gates. Once inside, I followed my Officer to a steep flight of concrete steps. It seemed a very long way down. In fact it was a total of 149 steps - I counted them many times after that day. We came to a steel-lined tunnel. Workmen were everywhere, installing what seemed to be miles of cables and wires. It was like being in another world. Initially, I felt a little claustrophobic, but that quickly passed when I discovered the immense size of the complex. There were: large rooms with plotting tables; small tunnel-shaped rooms equipped with teleprinters and switchboards; offices with desks and filing cabinets; a Galley and Wardroom; dormitories and washrooms; and from the noise of workmen constantly drilling and banging, there was obviously still much to be done.
It seemed very clear to me then, that we could all survive down there for quite a considerable time, if it ever became necessary. I also remember thinking that we would be very safe, away from the bombing of the City of Portsmouth.
I was fortunate to live at home with my parents in a quiet suburb (Cosham) of Portsmouth and travelled up and down Portsdown Hill each day on a Service bus. There were so many military personnel at the various Portsdown Hill Forts of Nelson, Purbrook, Southwick and Widley that if I missed the bus home and began to walk, a car would soon stop to offer a lift. We always wore our uniform and (unlike these modern times) it was quite safe to walk alone - even in the 'black-out'.

However, I was quite wrong in thinking we would be free from bombing on the Hill. Many nights when I was on duty and had to go up to the upper 'citadel' offices, the monotonous drone of German planes could be heard overhead (we used to call them 'moaning minnie's'). On these occasions the anti-aircraft fire from the Batteries was quite deafening. I recall one night in particular, when flares were dropped from the German planes.

* *I am indebted to Patricia Blandford for permission to quote from her Dissertation 'Fort Southwick What Useful Purpose Did It Serve'.*

Major General Guingand lecturing, apparently about the delights of Caen.
THE IWM H39732

Even if one had the petrol coupons, it became increasingly difficult to make coastal journeys. A forgotten identity card could cause a 'heap' of trouble.
THE NEWS

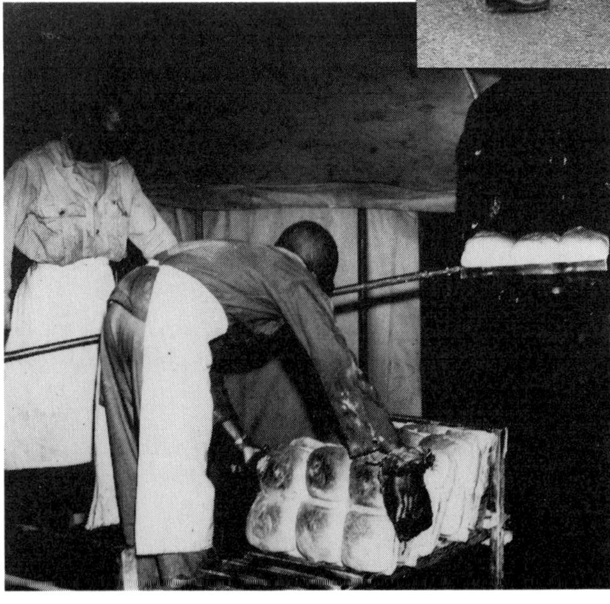

These American GI cooks were based at the Boys Technical School, Hilsea. Most 'native Brits' had never seen a coloured person before and their arrival caused quite a stir in neighbouring Cosham High St.
THE NEWS

> They hung like long, glittering ribbons, lighting up the area along the Hill and down below in Portchester, where the bombs were to fall. This made me think that the enemy knew something important about this area. Maybe they were aiming for Fort Nelson, which was an ammunition store.
> There were brighter moments and always a great sense of camaraderie. We had many happy times at social gatherings at the Golden Lion, Southwick, where the front bar, known as the 'Blue Room', had been unofficially adopted as an 'Officers' Mess'. The locals were wonderful people and always very polite. They went about their daily business as though we weren't there.'

Note: Later chapters include more reminisces from this lady's memories.

The Forts

These fascinating insights into the Fort Southwick 'goings on', reminds me to point out that all the Victorian Portsdown Forts, as well as most of the other Palmerston Forts at Wallington, Fareham and Gosport, were put to excellent use during the Second World War. You will notice that the lady in question lived in Cosham, so could go home every night. But most women operating the switchboards, who couldn't be accommodated at Fort Southwick, such as those belonging to the ATS section of the Royal Corp of Signals, were billeted at Fort Widley and 'bused to work'. To the west of the heights was Fort Nelson, utilised as an armoury and munitions store. So, decades after their original construction, for an event and role that never came to pass, these Palmerston Follies were pressed into service in the relentless pursuit of the most important wartime objective in the history of warfare.

Returning to the search for a suitable south coast headquarters, SHAEF argued that the location should preferably be as close as possible to Fort Southwick. As Southwick Mansion was already occupied by the Navy, not surprisingly it was shortlisted. The decision to actually select Southwick House was made in January 1944. It is reported (apart from the necessary considerations of availability, ease of communications, location and space) that the item which tipped the choice in Southwick's favour (*if that is the correct sentiment?*) was the excellent, extensive tree cover. It was reasoned that in spring and summer, the foliage would successfully camouflage the Mansion and encircling grounds and that the trees 'in full leaf' would allow ample cover for the tents and caravans required by the 21st Army Group and the Supreme Allied Commander. Thus, Southwick's place in the Second World War 'hall of fame' was assured. Incidentally, this 'forest' of trees was largely left in place until 1950, when a 'notable deforestation took place'. Sounds nasty!

The Final Choice of the HQ is... Southwick Mansion

Between June 1943 and early 1944 the House and its immediate surrounds had been subjected to a comparatively leisurely programme of alterations. But once the selection had been made, once Southwick Mansion was selected as the OVERLORD HQ, then a

A dinner parade at Hilsea.
THE NEWS

Dispatch Riders at Southwick. I'm not sure about the central character. Is he smiling?
THE NEWS

Meanwhile King George VI inspects a Naval Guard.
THE NEWS

frantic escalation of the construction programme was put in hand. Originally, access to Southwick House was via any one of seven Lodges (*See* Illus 3). The Mansion's 'front entrance' was through a High St pair of gates straddled by Church Lodge and the Church. Despite this, the Navy adopted Drove Road and Drove Lodge as their entrance - it had been for use by the servants! Thus, Drove Lodge became the main guardhouse. A major 'advantage' was that this route passed by the Golden Lion.

Entrances

Up until 1943, the stable block had remained almost unaltered, apart from the installation of a .22 rifle range in the upper hay loft. The internal destruction, necessary to accommodate the various models and plotting rooms, was completed between October 1943 and June 1944. A family retainer appears to have remained 'in residence' until this demolition work started. Perhaps the saddest alteration of all was the dismantling of the Mansion's brewery, in order to install a mock-up of a warship's bridge and bridge plotting room. A nice touch was that the copper vessel, which had not fermented any beer since the turn of the century, was donated to the Golden Lion brewery. The training models had to be put into use immediately, even whilst building work was continuing apace, and with no heating. Needless to say, lessons during the 1943 winter took place in greatcoats!

The Expulsion of the Navigation School

As the pace hotted up, ironically, the Navigation School, the 'original Trojan Horse', was moved to Greenwich, London, to make way for the D-Day 'mob'. This transfer took place by the 3rd April 1944. The AITC (Action Information Training Centre) section was left *in situ*. Not only were they effectively separated from the main house, but the sheer size and complexity of the completed models made their removal rather too difficult a task. The Spinney was replaced by concrete and buildings. A Meteorological Office Nissen hut (to be replaced by a brick-built guard house) was erected north of the Clock Tower, on the edge of the path to North Cross. This 'met-hut' was where the invasion weather maps were prepared. They were to prove vital to Eisenhower in his making the decision to delay and then launch the D-Day invasion fleet. Referring back to the Clock Tower, this building of pleasant architectural form had been utilised as 'a shot pheasant hanging room' by Col Evelyn's gamekeepers, right up to the navy takeover of the Mansion. Probably every inch of space was required, for the 'game' Squire's year-round daily breakfast was a pheasant's leg on a slice of toast.

A 'Met' Office Is Installed

A path was cut through the previously unpassable grove of shrubs and trees that separated the old stable block courtyard from the front of the Mansion, a forecourt was laid down and the establishment flag mast erected. The White Ensign was first raised on the flagpole for Admiral Ramsay, in April 1944. A large batch of 40

Further Alterations

'If you went down to the woods today....'
Creech Woods, as other woodlands in the Southwick area, were full to overflowing with camps of men waiting for a 'fast boat' to France.
THE NEWS

Some played cards,...

...others queued in the tea parade,...
THE NEWS

...whilst some simply lay about.
THE NEWS

Nissen Huts Appear

Nissen huts were hastily erected in the paddock alongside the Old Spinney, all the way from the stable courtyard to North Cross. Additionally, the *Frobisher* and *Dampier* buildings, in addition to two huts of *Scott Block* were laid down.

As mentioned, the Mansion, when requisitioned by the sailors, relied on a combination of wells and roof tanks for the supply of water. A rudimentary electricity supply was 'powered' by a generator and bank of batteries. The latter had been installed in the Spinney after the First World War and were maintained by a Mr Mackenzie, the Estate's full-time electrician. Goodness knows what and where the sewage was routed but I suspect cesspits and septic tanks were the means by which effluent was disposed. Whatever, on the navy's arrival, the various services required urgent modification. The impending influx of all the additional personnel associated with the OVERLORD teams, necessitated even more attention to be given to the power, water, drainage and telecommunication systems.

The Move Completed

During the weeks of April and May the various Command structures were to depart their original, scattered headquarters to move into Southwick House. The Navigation School had all departed by the 3rd April and Admiral Ramsay, Allied Naval Commander Expeditionary Force, moved in on the 26th April 1944. Three weeks later so did General Eisenhower, the Supreme Commander, and General Montgomery, Commander of the land forces.

The Generals ('Ike' & 'Monty') contemplate a rapid-fire carbine.
THE IWM NYP18650

Whilst 'the chaps' settle in to the wilds of Southwick Park.

Major Gen White has one foot on the ladder of his caravan,...
THE IWM H39151

...as does Brig Neville.
THE IWM H39160

Elsewhere, Major Gen White and his staff pose for a group photograph.
THE IWM H39153

Chapter 5
The Village's D-Day Build-Up 1944

Dispositions In The House & Park

The Supreme Commander, General Eisenhower parked his huge 'trailer home' alongside Pitymoor Lane, close to Pinsley Lodge. Until comparatively recently the hardpad of concrete was still evident. Admiral Ramsay and his ANCXF were scattered throughout Southwick House. General Montgomery (in his famous caravan), and a HQ staff of 20 officers and 200 men were billeted in mobile homes and under canvas in Southwick Park grounds, as were the HQ of the 21st Army Command. Mind you, a lot of Southwick Park seems to have been littered with caravans and tents. Vice-Admiral Schofield in his book* relates an incident, in 1944, concerning a Major General whose mobile home was deeply ensconced in a shrubbery wilderness. He woke up one morning to find that the Royal Marines, entrusted with the increased security, had completely barbed wired him in his lair. He was only calmed down when it was explained, his camouflage was so good that the Marines had failed to see him! Sounds a likely story to me.

Broomfield House & Monty's Guests

Despite 'Monty's' Southwick Park presence, he was also resident and holding court at Broomfield House. Here he entertained a number of eminent visitors to dinner, in the lead-up to the invasion. Guests included King George VI, Prime Minister Churchill, General Smuts of South Africa, as well as Dominion Premiers and Colonial luminaries, amongst which were Mr Mackenzie King of Canada, Peter Fraser of New Zealand and Sir Godfrey Huggins of Southern Rhodesia. It appears that 'Monty' was keen to take bets proffered in the general run of after dinner conversation. Should someone express an opinion coupled with a wager on, for instance, when

The Wagers

**With acknowledgements to 'Navigation and Direction The Story of HMS Dryad' by Vice Admiral B B Schofield, published by Kenneth Mason, Emsworth.*

In the grounds of The Park it was possible for a couple of Brigadiers (Duke and Mackillop) to have a quick conference.
THE IWM H39173

'Ike' and 'Monty' have a fireside chat.
THE IWM 13912189

Monty 'pressing' flesh in Portsmouth
THE NEWS

the war would end, who would get to which war objective first or which political party would win the post-war election, then 'Monty' pulled out the betting book and recorded the matter. This predilection to have a bet is a strange quirk, for not only did Montgomery plan military strategy so there were no gambles, nothing but certainty, but he neither drank alcohol or smoked.

'Shooting-up' the Tree

Only a few years ago a venerable tree was taken down at Broomfield House. The forester experienced a problem with his saw, as if the cutting edge was striking metal. Once the tree was felled, it could be seen that the outer rings were peppered with bullets, which turned out to be machine gun slugs. It is rumoured that, after particularly lively meals, 'Monty' and 'Ike' were inclined to wander into the garden and 'shoot-up' the tree in question.

D-Day Inconveniences...

Following the decision to make Southwick House the OVERLORD Headquarters, at and from which all the D-Day planning would be implemented and the landings launched, the events surrounding the weeks of April, May and June were to have an enormous impact on the residents of the village. Mind you, most of the inhabitants of the United Kingdom were equally inconvenienced during those few months. It was during this period that the countrymen of this 'sceptred isle' were to lose even those few freedoms left to the average wartime household. Draconian measures prohibited any movement in a ten mile wide coastal strip, all the way from the Wash down to Lands End. This was in addition to a large tract of Scottish coastline and innumerable areas being temporarily used as vehicle parks, camps, airfields and ammunition dumps. On the 10th March personal travel, as well as most mail and telephone contacts were severely restricted. On the 6th April all military leave was curtailed. To follow were unheard of restrictions in respect of foreign embassies, diplomats, their rights of movement, diplomatic bags and privileges. Travel to and from Southern Ireland, where German agents were free to move around without let or hindrance, was temporarily stopped. On the other hand, the Generals were engaged in much travel and flesh-pressing. General Montgomery was to review many operational units in the area and dropped in on the Fort Southwick UGHQ.

& Restrictions

Security Leaks

As the tempo increased and D-Day inexorably approached, the Mansion was cordoned off. The only reported local leak in security was perpetrated by the wife of a naval petty officer, living close by the village shop, who wrote to her husband to say she 'saw Monty today'. The censor spotted this breach of regulations and the lady was severely reprimanded. At least that slip-up was not on the scale of an American Sergeant based in London. In error, he managed to post his sister in the USA a package of OVERLORD documents, which spilled out in a Chicago postal sorting office when the

DAILY EXPRESS MONDAY JUNE 12 1944

DAILY EXPRESS Opinion

The mood

THE Churchill warning against over-optimism has been duly delivered in the constituencies over the week-end.

It has served rather to underline and emphasise the dominant mood of the people than to correct it.

If it were possible to dig into the minds of the people of these islands, you would find good hope and sober confidence, and a fierce eagerness for news, and yet more news.

But little enough of wild rejoicing over victories yet unwon, no willingness to prophesy—and most certainly no feeling that Victory is already there for the plucking.

The bridgehead is a triumph. It forms the basis of the main battle that is still to be fought against the German armies. It is not the battle itself.

The mood today is one of thankfulness; the cheering has been saved for a later date.

Russian attack

ONCE again the Red armies are on the move. Again the enemy gives the first news of Russian attack, and again Stalin's Order of the Day is delayed. When it comes it tells of a wide breach torn in the enemy's line and a decisive Russian advance.

This time the point of attack was unexpected, most of all by the Finns, who thought seven German divisions inside their country were a greater danger than the Russian armies massed on the border.

The start

THE Finns misread the signs in 1941. There was some excuse for mistakes by satellite opportunists in the floodtide of German success.

There was none in the spring of this year when Finland had the chance to get out on easy terms.

Now, in the Karelian Isthmus, Finnish armies take the first consequences of their leaders' blunder and blindness.

They receive the first, and only the first, of the blows that are coming from the east. Russia's resources are now so immense that she, too, can strike north, south and centre.

Rout in Italy

IN this tremendous week great victories, which at any other time would have resounded through the land, have passed with scarcely a comment, as the world kept its eyes on the Normandy beachheads.

A week ago the fall of Rome was announced. To-day the armies that sought to hold the capital are split in two.

Sixty miles north of the capital, Alexander's pursuing forces sweep through Montalto, while in the east Orsogna falls, Pescara falls, and Kesselring's retreat is become a rout.

Climax

MILITARILY, this great pursuit of the Germans, first up the shin, and then up the calf of Italy is the climax and fruition of Alexander's campaign, even more than was the fall of Rome.

For here is the shining evidence that the beaten German has no stomach for a fight. He stood on the Velletri-Valmontone line while he could. But it was his last fling in Southern and Central Italy.

Even yet the full importance of this victory is not revealed. But, in the tense days that are ahead, the memory of this week of triumph after victory is worth storing up.

It will happen again on another front.

Supermen

BRITAIN should be proud of her men of science and grateful for their courage as well as their brains.

They have backed up the soldier, the sailor and the airman magnificently throughout this war. And now here they are, ahead of the invading armies, picking up sand samples under the noses of the German sentries from the very beaches to be attacked.

In countering the magnetic mine, in devising new and still more powerful bombs and projectiles, in developing radiolocation, in pioneering the anti-aircraft rocket and the rocket ships and planes, they have left their opposite numbers in Germany hopelessly out of the race.

Civilian salute to Two Commanders

1 Letter from home to EISENHOWER

General Dwight Eisenhower,
Supreme Headquarters
in England.

NEW YORK, Sunday.

DEAR GENERAL,—In case you don't know it, you are now America's No. 1 hero. They have already named a street after you, and they did not do that even for General Douglas MacArthur.

Yes, the street where you were born—Day-street in Denison, Texas—is soon going to be known as Eisenhower-street. And I bet you can't guess why America has taken you so completely to its heart.

No, it is not just because you are leading this great invasion upon which your countrymen, in common with mine, have placed such great hopes. It is much more because amid all the loftiness of the place which history has chosen for you, you have shown that you are still what they call a very human guy.

★

Remember you were asked on D Day morning how you felt after you had said "Let's go"? Well, you answered: "I'm so goldurn nervous I'm boiling over."

Americans liked that spontaneous, unaffected remark.

It showed them that, despite everything that has happened to you, you still react like one of them.

It was just what they were thinking.

Everyone was surprised here at what has happened since D Day. Your country has the reputation, you know, for putting on a show. Everyone was expecting something like a Boat-race night used to be in London back in the good old days.

There was some reason for it. There had been some wild scenes after that fake invasion report on the pre-D Day Saturday afternoon. But it did not come this time.

★

America today is as sober as if it had only just gone to war. They say that thousands of people who have not been inside of a church since they were married have gone to pray for you and the men, British as well as American, under you during these past days.

And with my own eyes I saw the disgust that greeted two drunks in a New York restaurant last night after they had proclaimed that their condition was to be blamed upon their exhilaration over the invasion.

No, these are serious days. You can get a ringside table at almost any New York night club these days, and you have probably heard what the night life here had been up to D Day.

And even in Los Angeles, which is 6,000 miles away from your beachheads, cinema attendances have fallen off as much as 40 per cent.

It is not that there is any defeatism felt about this great operation which you have started. There is sober confidence and complete trust in you and the great English-speaking army of liberation with which you have surrounded yourself.

No, I think the answer is that for millions of Americans this is the beginning of the war.

It has been a long way off until now. Not for New Mexico, of course, which lost its flower at Bataan, or for a family here and a family there who looked towards a jungle grave in the Pacific Isle or to a rough cross under an olive tree in Italy. But for the great masses, yes.

★

Their boys had been within the security of Britain, writing home of the good times they were having, of the interesting things they were seeing.

And now suddenly there are no more letters. Everyone sees his or her son fighting the battle like the Russians have fought. It has wrought a great change in America. Life goes on seemingly as usual, but underneath it doesn't.

"FIELD MARSHAL ROMMEL, I PRESUME"

2 Doris wrote in her exercise book:-

'The King came to see Monty'

by PAUL HOLT

H.Q., 21ST ARMY GROUP, IN THE FIELD, Sunday.

TO find the address from which this is written needs skill. Now you see it, now you don't. It's a matter of luck.

To prove those words I have only to add that during the past seven days on seven journeys to General Montgomery's headquarters I have not once been stopped, challenged or asked to show my credentials. It has been enough that I knew the way.

But if I were to be talking now instead of writing, and a man asked me, I think I would reply, in the words of that famous yokel: "If I were you I wouldn't start from here."

It is a queer journey to Monty. Up a hill and down a hill, and maybe at the point you need to turn off there will be a waiting convoy, with dreaming soldiers sitting at the wheels. And next time there is a woman with a perambulator waiting for the wave of a redcap soldier to cross against the flow of Shermans or Churchills. Which she soon gets.

A siren

UP a lane and there is one more solitary redcap, swing in a gateway and there is a little tent on the drive up to a pretty Georgian house. An empty tent.

In front of it, though, a warlike emblem. Two feet of steel tubing, painted red and blue, hangs from a dainty gibbet and there is a steel rod, red and blue too, with which to strike this modest and rural air raid warning.

Beyond that there is peace again.

A rusty gravel drive towards an old porch in the shade. And at the back those square honest Georgian windows, revealing a hint of mahogany and chintz and china cats indoors. And a scruffy lawn that will turn brown soon under the sun.

Beyond there is the blue-grey of new-mown hay and quiet copses. One strand of barbed wire that would not check a poacher, let alone a paratroop. It is vague and old and full of that misty Sunday peace.

And here is the great man.

Your pardon. I have found that most of General Montgomery's staff officers never mention his name. They call him the great man. They say "The great man wants you", "The great man is coming". The tag has just that edge needed by real English affection.

Subtle man

HE strolls out from the house feeling with his gentle grey hands that have large knuckles for the neck of his shrunken grey sweater.

I have learned one thing already. If he plans to stay put he will wear battledress. If he is going places across the water he will wear his grey sweater and corduroy trousers.

The great man is subtle.

When I met him on D Day he gestured in apology to his country Sunday afternoon wear and said: "This is how I dress when I go fighting." He was right. For all his seeming leisure, within hours he was in a ship off the coast of Normandy.

Is this the H.Q. 21st Army Group, heart of the assault on France? I couldn't know. There is only one telephone, which rings infrequently. Out of one window you may see a young, plumping Guards colonel with greying hair, who chats with a small group of junior Canadian and American officers on the lawn.

Would you say so?

He will return

BE sure of one thing. The great man will return here. Over this week-end he has set up his battle headquarters in France to direct in person the battle of the first counter attack which should by rights be starting soon. Dispositions for that battle made with his field commanders, he will come back.

A year ago when the final assault on Tunis had begun I found the great man in Cairo, where he had flown to read the Lessons in the cathedral on Sunday morning.

Let's try again for these elusive army headquarters. Would this be it? The scent is warmer. In a village main street I see a full admiral entering the tobacco sweets and flypapers shop of Mrs. —— (name censored). He has been working with the American Navy, to be sure, for he asks for a tin of Edgworth pipe tobacco.

There are Wrens at the corner by the church, showing their very short gym shorts under the blue macs.

Clearly the young ladies of the cypher and communications department of H.Q. 21 A.G.

The villagers take no notice, politely going about their business and their gossip.

Round the corner in a lane a clutch of crash-helmeted despatch riders chew gum and brood astride their violent machines. The redcap on point duty is talking about the weather to an angular woman in tweeds escorted by two sad spaniels.

The schoolroom might give a clue. A vast, spectacled American major, all got up for battle like Frankenstein's monster, has a roll of maps under his arm.

To enter the asphalt playground a security officer is asked personally to vouch for you. The children sit on a bench at the other end of the yard like so many budgerigars, chattering in whispers.

Inside the one schoolroom a general is sitting on the cold iron stove under a print showing Boy Cornwell, V.C.,** at his gun. A brigadier is reading with deep attention a half-rubbed-out chalk Bible quotation which is annotated 1.5.44.

Over the map of the world, with the British Empire in dying red, has been pinned the map of France on which a security officer is up-dating exact positions of our forces, German forces, German floodings.

An Essay

WHILE I am waiting for the great man, or the "senior staff officer," who will be talking at today's conference, I open the little desk that so hurts my knees.

It belongs to Doris Mills (false name). I'd like to meet her. On Wednesday she wrote in her exercise book: Essay. What I did today. It was a lovely day. We did not work in the afternoon. The King came to see Monty. I had a nice dinner.

"We did not work in the afternoon," wrote Doris. The brigadier in charge of this daily conference, from which the world learns the course of the battle that decides the fate of the world, is worried about Doris' out to play.

Two days ago he said: "Gentlemen. Education must go on, as well as battles. I think we shall have to hold this conference later in the afternoon. I have spoken to the Commander-in-Chief about it and he agrees. Shall we say 4.15—er—that is, sixteen hours fifteen?"

After the captains have departed daily a few giant security police enter silently with soft tread to pick up every scrap of paper that may have been screwed and thrown on the floor.

But they don't touch Doris's exercise book.

Invisible

THE essence of this invasion coast and headquarters scene is the huge good manners of both military and locals. Politely they ignore each other.

The people don't come out when Monty goes by. They pretend they never saw him.

** John Travers Cornwell, Boy First Class Royal Navy aged 16, was posthumously awarded V.C. for his share in Battle of Jutland. He stood at his post "in a most exposed part," with a dead and dying gun crew around him, quietly awaiting orders. He was mortally wounded.

WILLIAM HICKEY
Love rah-rah

SINCE most people get a lot of fun out of glancing through the agony columns and matrimonial advertisements of British newspapers and magazines from time to time I want to tell you today about a rather more ambitious enterprise conducted along the same lines in Mexico City. […]

Rupert and the Blue Mountain—9

Looking up at Bill's cry, Rupert sees that their friend the old Professor is approaching. […]

BY the WAY
by Beachcomber

THE story of the husband who, the other day, found his wife's too intimate friend hiding up the chimney reminded me of the foolish girl who became the 37th wife of a certain Eastern gentleman. The junior member of the harem, noticing her lord's coldness, said pathetically, "Abdul, is there someone else?" […]

The sterling area

The Memoirs of Foulenough

A new musical note

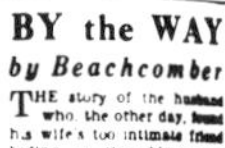

CROSSWORD

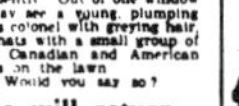

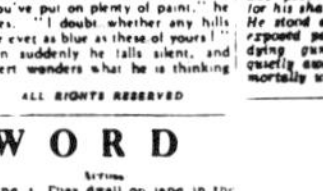

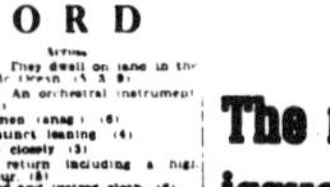

RADIO

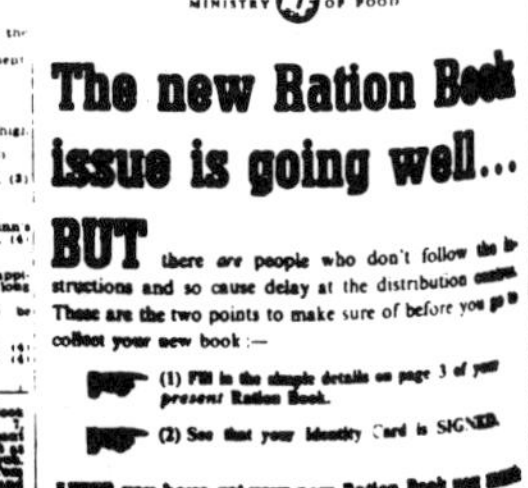

envelope burst open. Another American of a senior rank, who had been a youthful colleague of Eisenhower, and probably one or three cocktails too far in, whilst at a London hotel party, bragged about the D-Day date. Despite his illustrious (erstwhile) chum, he was dispatched home in purdah and *sans rank*.

The article reprinted below appeared in the *Daily Express* of Monday June 12th 1944 and gives an idea of the circumspection required in even describing the location of and atmosphere at the 'Invasion' headquarters. And this was up to a week after the invasion had taken place!

Doris wrote in her exercise book:-

THE KING CAME TO SEE MONTY

by Paul Holt

HQ, 21st Army Group in The Field, Sunday

To find the address from which this is written needs skill. Now you see it, now you don't. It's a matter of luck.

To prove those words I have only to add that during the past seven days on seven journeys to General Montgomery's headquarters I have not once been stopped, challenged, or asked to show my credentials. It has been enough that I knew the way.

But if I were to be talking now instead of writing, and a man asked me. I think I would reply, in the words of that famous yokel, 'If I were you, I wouldn't start from here'.

It is a queer journey to Monty. Up a hill and down a hill, and maybe at the point you need to turn off there will be a waiting convoy, with dreaming soldiers sitting at the wheels. And next time there is a woman with a perambulator waiting for the wave of a redcap soldier to cross against the flow of Shermans or Churchill [*tanks*]. Which she soon gets.

A siren

Up a lane and there is one more solitary redcap, swing in a gateway and there is a little tent on the drive up to a pretty Georgian house. An empty tent.

In front of it though is a warlike emblem. Two feet of steel tubing, painted red and blue, hangs from a dainty gibbet, and there is a steel rod, red and blue too with which to strike this modest and rural air raid warning.

Beyond that there is peace again.

A rustly gravel drive towards an old Porch in the shade. And at the back those square honest Georgian windows, revealing a hint of mahogany and chintz and china cats indoors. And a scruffy lawn that will turn brown soon under the sun.

Beyond there is blue-grey of new mown hay and quiet copses. One strand of barbed wire that would not check a poacher let alone a paratroop. It is vague and old and full of that misty Sunday peace.

And here is the great man.

Your pardon. I have found that most of General Montgomery's staff officers never mention his name. They call him the great man. They say: 'The great man wants you'; 'The great man is coming'. The tag has just that edge needed by real English affection.

Life at Broomfield House in May 1944 was very busy, with much coming and going of the important and very important.
Here, King George VI poses beside Gen Montgomery's famous caravan. The shield depicts Monty's victorious North African campaigns at Egypt, Tripoli, Tunis and Sicily.
THE IWM H38734

Here the King and 'Monty' stroll in the grounds of Broomfield House.
THE IWM H38742

Prime Minister Winston Churchill in his siren suit...
THE IWM H38661

...and in rather more formal gear.
THE IWM H38660

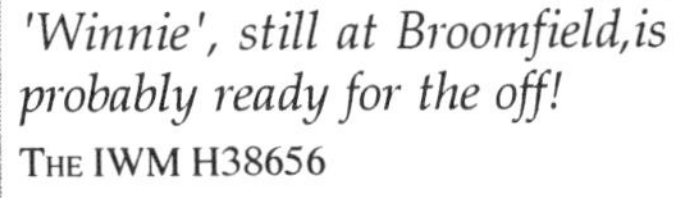

'Winnie', still at Broomfield,is probably ready for the off!
THE IWM H38656

Subtle man

He strolls out from the house feeling, with his gentle grey hands that have large knuckles, for the neck of his shrunken grey sweater.
I have learned one thing already. If he plans to stay put he will wear battledress. If he is going places across the water he will wear his grey sweater and corduroy trousers.
The great man is subtle.
When I met him on D-Day he gestured in apology to his country Sunday afternoon wear and said: 'This is how I dress when I go fighting'. He was right. For all his seeming leisure, within hours he was in a ship off the coast of Normandy.
Is this the HQ 21st Army Group heart of the assault on France? I couldn't know. There is only one telephone, which rings infrequently. Out of one window you may see a young, plumping Guards Colonel with greying hair, who chats with a small group of junior Canadian and American officers on the lawn. Would you say so?

He will return

Be sure of one thing. The great man will return here. Over this week-end he has set up his battle headquarters in France to direct in person the battle of the first counter-attack, which should by rights be starting soon. Dispositions for that battle made with his Field Commanders, he will come back.
A year ago, when the final assault on Tunis had begun, I found the great man in Cairo, where he had flown to read the Lessons in the Cathedral on Sunday morning.
Let's try again for these elusive army headquarters. Would this be it? The scent is warmer. In a village main street I see a full admiral entering the tobacco, sweets and flypapers shop for Mrs... (name censored). He has been working with the American Navy, to be sure, for he asks for a tin of Edgworth pipe tobacco.
There are Wrens at the corner by the Church, showing their very short gym shorts under the blue macs.
Clearly the young ladies of the cypher and communications department of HQ21 (Army Group). The villagers take no notice, politely going about their business and their gossip.
Round the corner, in a lane, a clutch of crash-helmeted despatch riders chew gum and brood astride their violent machines. The redcap on point duty is talking about the weather to an angular woman in tweeds escorted by two sad spaniels.
The schoolroom might give a clue. A vast, bespectacled American major, all got up for battle like Frankenstein's monster has a roll of maps under his arm.
To enter the asphalt playground a security officer is asked personally to vouch for you. The children sit on a bench at the other end of the yard like so many budgerigars, chattering in whispers. Inside the one schoolroom a general is sitting on the cold iron stove under a print showing Boy Cornwell, VC, at his gun+. A brigadier is reading with deep attention a half-rubbed-out chalk Bible quotation which is annotated 1.5.44.

+ John Travers Cornwell, Boy, First Class Royal Navy, aged 16 1/2, was posthumously awarded the V.C. for his share in the Battle of Jutland (1916). He stood at his post 'in a most exposed part', with a dead and dying gun crew around him, quietly awaiting orders. He was mortally wounded (early in the action)

The Canadian Prime Minister Mr Mackenzie King, pays a visit on 'Monty' at Broomfield,...
The IWM H38655

...as does New Zealand's Prime Minister, Mr Peter Fraser.
The IWM H38772

Winston and 'Monty' walk the grounds of Southwick House, dodging the camouflage concealing the 'tented city' in the Park.
The IWM H38657

Gen Eisenhower inspecting his countrymen. On this occasion he is supposed to have said "God help the Nazis if you fight as well as you train".
The IWM EA15099

Admiral Sir Bertram Ramsey and Gen Eisenhower leaving a 21st Army Group conference - 'snapped' outside the main entrance of Southwick House.
The IWM H39152

Never one for tittle-tattle, I can only advise that this is Miss Kay Summersby. She was Eisenhower's personal driver in North Africa, Italy and the UK. Thank goodness there weren't portable telephones in those far off days).
The IWM H39155

Over the map of the world, with the British Empire in dying red, has been pinned the map of France on which a security Officer is up-dating exact positions of our forces, German forces. (and) German floodings.

An Essay

While I am waiting for the great man, or the 'senior staff officer' who will be talking at today's conference, I open the little desk that so hurts my knees.
It belong to Doris Mills (false name). I'd like to meet her. On Wednesday she wrote in her exercise book: Essay. What I did today. It was a lovely day. We did not work in the afternoon. The King came to see Monty. I had a nice dinner.
'We did not work in the afternoon, 'wrote Doris. The brigadier in charge of this daily conference, from which the world learns the course of the battle that decides the fate of the world, is worried about Doris out to play.
Two days ago he said: 'Gentlemen. Education must go on, as well as battles. I think we shall have to hold this conference later in the afternoon. I have spoken to the Commander-in-Chief about it, and he agrees. Shall we say 4.15- er -that is sixteen hours fifteen?'
After the captains have departed, daily, a few giant security police enter silently with soft tread to pick up every scrap of paper that may have been screwed and thrown on the floor.
But they don't touch Doris's exercise book.

Invisible

The essence of this invasion coast and headquarters scene is the huge good manners of both military and locals. Politely they ignore each other.
The people don't come out when Monty goes by. They prefer to pretend they never saw him.

With acknowledgements to the Express Newspaper Group for permission to reprint the article and reproduce the page.

The WRNS tale (cont):

More Of The Wren's Tale

I made frequent trips to Southwick House, which had been taken over by the Navy, to train switchboard personnel. Red-capped Military Police were everywhere and it was quite obvious that something special was going on. In early spring 1944, large numbers of vehicles and men were coming into the area. A friend told me of the day that she had seen soldiers in full kit scaling the chalk-pit (Later I realised why).
As a Second Officer WRNS in charge of the telephone switchboards, I attended a briefing where I was told that the new Radio Wireless on which we had been training, was to be used by our lads who would be crossing the channel to France, to rescue Servicemen trapped on the beaches of Normandy.
This secret operation was called 'Operation Overlord' and I remember feeling a great sense of pride at being so closely connected with it and also in knowing that just to the North of us were the headquarters of General Eisenhower and General Montgomery, planning this massive Operation.
We all felt very honoured when Montgomery visited us on several occasions at UGHQ. I always felt rather in awe of him - he seemed a very

The Engineers create The Hardway near Gosport. Here were to be loaded many, many landing craft.
THE IWM H38572

The official caption reads 'Tons of Artillery shells stored in bays along a quiet country lane'. In fact, most of the lanes resembled armoured vehicle blighted motorways, with...
THE IWM AP15665

...tanks at Portchester...
THE NEWS

...and tanks at Horndean.
THE NEWS

> serious man indeed, and never smiled.
> Soon, tanks were parked along the roads, half-hidden in the hedgerows; it seemed as if every space in the countryside was filled with soldiers, tanks and equipment.'

The Map Room

During May part of a vast plywood wall map, covering the coastline from Calais to Brest, was installed in Southwick House, in the room now known as the Map Room. This had been constructed by the firm of Chad Valley Toys, a leading firm of children's toy manufacturers. Two workmen were duly despatched to deliver and install the item. Due to the strict security clamp down, they were not allowed to leave, being kept in the Mansion until after the Invasion was over. I don't expect anyone took the bother to explain that part of the mission to them, before they packed their tool bags! And imagine explaining that away to the little woman! If they felt hard done by, I am fairly certain that several craftsmen on board one of the fighting ships had to work on when the ship sailed. They had little choice but to unwittingly, and no doubt unwillingly, take part in the D-Day landings, not returning until the particular beach-head had been well and truly established.

Unwilling Participation

Daily staff conferences were held in the old library of the Mansion, which had become the south dining room. It is rumoured, whilst the security of the room was being checked out, that a hoard of gold pieces, dating back to the early 1800s was found on top of one of the library bookcases. I can well imagine an 18thC Thistlethwayte stashing away a few thousand coins, as insurance against the threat of invasion by the French. But what happened to the hord?

A 'Stash' of Gold

On the 8th May, Eisenhower chose the 5th June as the day on which to launch Operation OVERLORD. This date was reaffirmed on the 25th May, after orders had gone out on the 23rd May to make ready. The choice of dates was restricted to some 4-6 days per month, referred to as 'the windows'. This period was when the states of tide and sunrise were at their best for the project. The June 'windows' were the 5th to 7th and the 18th to 20th, with the early slot being the most propitious choice - as there would be a full moon. Apart from the logistical difficulties of keeping tens of thousands of men hanging about on boats and in and around hedgerows, the other pressing variables were those of time and weather.

The 5th June

The weather was an obvious consideration. It could critically affect the sea state and thus the operation of the landing craft, the minesweepers, channel markers, cable layers, as well as the ammunition, fuel and salvage ships. In addition to these prime deliberations, there were the vital projects of 'Mulberry' and 'PLUTO'. Mulberrys were artificial floating harbours originally a product of Churchill's fertile imagination. In essence each Mulberry Harbour

The Mulberry Harbours

It was very difficult not to bump into tanks, trucks and men, here at Stokes Bay.
The News

Some tank crew were lucky enough to be served a daily 'pinta',...
The IWM H38988

...others were given a flower!
The IWM H38989

Some took a break,...
The IWM H38986

...whilst others took the opportunity to do their 'doby'.
The News

was made up of a collection of enormous floating caissons of concrete and steel which had to be towed across the Channel. Enormous? Well, each individual caisson measured some 200ft x 55ft x 60ft high and weighed about 6,000 tons. There's big! Once linked together and tied into an outer breakwater of sunken ships and floating pierheads, the whole were to form two huge, prefabricated ports 'each as big as Dover'. From side to side the outer breakwaters were about 2 miles apart and the distance between the shore and the furthermost breakwater was approximately 1 mile. Their combined construction used up to 2 million tons of concrete and steelwork. Despite the enormous amounts of material they 'consumed' and the enormous manpower required (up to 55,000 bodies at the height of the programme), the overriding *raison d'etre* behind their planned deployment ensured a 'top priority' tag. Lessons learnt during earlier wartime experiences convinced the planners that the best method of pursuing the invasion was to bypass established, well defended ports and harbours, which might not fall into attacking forces hands for countless days. The wisdom of this line of thought, even if an extreme case, was borne out by the German submarine base of St Nazaire which was left to its own devices for many months, not surrendering until after the official end of the war. Conversely, rather than float, yet another vital civil engineering feat was that of PLUTO, or 'Pipe Line Under The Ocean', designed to sink to the sea-bed. The scheme enabled a considerable quantity of the invading forces fuel requirements to be piped underwater, all the way to the French coast. The initial pipes were laid from Lepe, near the mouth of Southampton Water, beneath the Solent to Gunard, on the Isle of Wight. From there, land pipes were routed to the south IOW seaside locations of Sandown and Shanklin. At each of these resorts, a pumping station pulsed the liquid to the Cherbourg peninsula, thus avoiding the chance of shipborne supplies being delayed or destroyed by enemy action. Machines simply will not operate without the 'fluence'!

PLUTO

The question of time not only involved the debilitating effects of the Allied troops being cooped up in the 'waiting room', or in this case in the confines of an assault landing craft. It also had to take account of what the Germans and their Axis allies were up to in their efforts to thwart the coming invasion. It was no secret to one and all that the shores of Europe were to experience a seaborne invasion - somewhere and 'somewhen'. The one million 'Deutschmark' question for the defending forces was when and where? This fascinating subject and the techniques of deception deployed to fool the Nazis is unfortunately outside the scope of this book, as Southwick was not a centre of the 'dirty-tricks' brigade. The difficulty for the Allied Commanders was that the longer the delay in putting into hand the Invasion, the more difficult it was to maintain the various

German Doubts

The waiting must have seemed endless. A hand of cards in the woods may well have seemed preferable to...
THE NEWS

...being 'holed up' ,as were these tank crews, near Paulsgrove...
THE IWM 1126/212

...or these squaddies cleaning up after 'tucker'.
THE NEWS

deceptions being used to conceal the actual plans. For instance, it only required one stray Luftwaffe reconnaissance plane to slip through the RAF's tight grip on the airspace over the Channel. If that were to occur, the massive build up of vessels (of every type and size imaginable) in the Solent waters, coupled with the vast camps of men and vehicles spread over the land bordering the Solent and the South Coast, could lead to only one conclusion. It would not require a leading strategist to realise 'the grand design'. To give an idea of the density of the assembled ships, the crews of the victualling vessels that set out daily from Royal Clarence Yard (on the Gosport side of Portsmouth Harbour) were '...of the opinion that it was damned near possible to hop from one ship to another, all the way from Portsmouth to the Isle of Wight, without getting ones feet wet.'

Rommel & The Atlantic Wall

In November 1943 Field-Marshal Erwin Rommel had been appointed to reorganise the defences of the Axis Atlantic Wall. The Allies were well aware that every month that passed, with the efficient Field Marshal at the helm, could cost hundreds or thousands more lives. Fortunately (for the Allies), despite the assurances of the propaganda machine, which appeared to exist solely to assuage Hitler's worries, Rommel found the facts depressingly short of the promises. The impregnability of the Atlantic Wall was like the Emperor's clothes - a figment of the Fuhrer's imagination. This fact was quickly appreciated by Rommel and other senior German officers. They demanded to be supplied with as much labour and materials as could be organised - and spared from other projects. Most importantly, they fervently prayed for as much time as possible.

The Flying Bombs

Another more ephemeral, if potentially infinitely more urgent reason for the Allies to allow as little delay as possible was revealed by intelligence gathering. This uncovered the unnerving fact that the Germans were working on a 'new' weapon, a pilotless aeroplane and or rocket, a flying bomb which was to 'come on stream' sometime in 1944. It was considered most likely that the Germans would target both Portsmouth and Southampton with these weapons, possibly capable of mass destruction. Incidentally, this prediction was subsequently discovered to be perfectly correct from captured enemy maps and plans. Their effect on the preparation for the D-Day landings can best be appreciated on considering General Eisenhower's thoughts that '...if Germany had perfected these new weapons earlier and targeted the Portsmouth-Southampton area, then Operation OVERLORD might well have had to be called off'. Mmh! In an effort to delay the production of these missiles, a spring bombing campaign was aimed at both the development centres and the proposed launching sites. In the event, the unsuspecting citizens of London Town became acquainted with the first V-1 flying

V-1s..

Whoops!
THE IWM CH12746

Scaffolding was pressed into service to erect embarkation pierheads at Southsea beach.
THE NEWS

Lining up amphibious troop carriers (known as DUKW) at The Hardway, Gosport.
THE NEWS

bomb (nicknamed 'doodle-bugs' due to their peculiar 'call note' as they plummeted to earth) on the 12th June 1944 - just 6 days after the D-Day invasion commenced. The more powerful and totally unheralded V-2 exploded on British soil on the 1st August. So that's why the invasion could not be allowed to slip from one month to the next!

& V-2s

A further pressure, if one was required, was emanating from Marshal Joseph Stalin. For quite some time the Americans and British Commanders had been browbeaten by 'old Joe' to launch an offensive, any old offensive, against the German forces holding down Western Europe. This was in order to relieve the enormous pressure on the Red Army troops in their desperate defence of Russian soil. Any delays, and there had been one or three, were viewed with a great deal of suspicion and resentment by our then Russian ally.

Marshal Stalin

Naturally, the security surrounding Operation OVERLORD was intense. Despite this, there were some raised eyebrows and extremely worried intelligence department personnel when the Daily Telegraph crossword puzzles of May and June were viewed. These contained the words *Mulberry*, *Neptune*, *Omaha* and *Overlord*. As it turned out their inclusion was nothing more than a truly amazing coincidence.

Further Security Lapses

In order to bring about the invasion, the build-up of men and machines gathered pace, taking on a momentum of its own making. To the inhabitants of the south coast counties it must have seemed as if every nook and cranny was filled with soldiers, tanks and trucks. Almost all the shady lanes, fields, copses and woods of the countryside surrounding Southwick were stacked high with the camps of men and and their equipment, as well as lorry and tank marshalling points and dumps of armoury. Very busy local army locations were Creech Woods, straddling Place Wood road, the Southwick to Denmead thoroughfare, and the various farmsteads scattered around its edges, such as Upper Beckford, Lower Beckford and Creech Farms. By about May the troop dispositions in the area included the:

3rd Canadian Div. spread from Chilworth (half way between Southampton and Romsey) east as far as Stokes Bay, Gosport, and to land at JUNO Beach-head. One of their Armoured Regiments was at Gosport;

231st Brigade at Fawley & Hythe and to land at GOLD Beach-head;

3rd British Div. & 27th Armoured Brigade spread on a front from the north of Portsmouth around through Waterlooville to Emsworth, and to land at SWORD Beach-head. Their 48th Commando group were at Southampton Common, the 7th Armoured Div. lined the A3 from The George Inn, Widley, to Horndean and the 2nd Battalion East Yorks Regt. were camped

All aboard... or more accurately 'all change', for this is the 'Droxford Halt' of the Dominion Premier's War Cabinet, in early June 1944. From left to right are Mr Mackenzie King (Canada), Winston Churchill (in his rompers), Mr Peter Fraser (New Zealand), Gen Eisenhower of the USA (one of our 'mislaid' colonies), Sir Godfrey Huggins (Southern Rhodesia) and Gen Smuts (South Africa).
THE IWM H38457

General de Gaulle and 'Ike', with Winston Churchill in the background.
THE IWM EA25478

The 'upper brass' gather in ever-increasing numbers, here outside the main entrance of Southwick House.
THE IWM H39165

at Waterlooville.
At Roche Court Estate, north of Fareham, were a Canadian Tank Brigade and a Signals Unit. (This site had been gifted to Southwick Priory in 1384 and was to be bought back into the Southwick Estate by Squire Borthwick-Norton in 1949. *Plus ca change*!)

Hidden away at the Denmead end of Creech Woods, on the east side of Place Wood road was a quite extensive brick built camp. The site is still just distinguishable by the outline of various groundworks and foundations in amongst the forest of pine trees. One favourable spin-off, resulting from the sheer volume of amoured vehicles, was that Place Wood road was widened and resurfaced to cope with the unprecedented flow and weight of traffic. The sharp corners were concreted to cope with the destructive effects of tank tracks when spinning. Another relic of those days is the vehicle passing and turning point at the bottom of the steep dip (in the Southwick to Denmead road), just beyond Boulter Lane, close by Assells Row.

Some More Of The Wren's Tale

The WRNS tale (cont):

> 'By the first day in June men were sitting in convoys of parked vehicles - some sprawled in groups on the grass playing cards. Others were writing letters, presumable to their loved ones. They all seemed in very good spirits and would wave as we drove past.'

The Meon Valley Railway

The now discontinued Meon Valley Railway connected with a main line near Alton. It ran down the length of the picturesque River Meon valley passing through Tisted, Privett, West Meon, Droxford and Wickham *en route* to Fareham. The line was extensively employed during the invasion build-up in order to transport machinery, mines and troops. Without doubt, the most significant event in the railway's history was its involvement in the D-Day planning, for it was in a railway siding at Droxford station that a War Cabinet of the Americans, British and Dominion Premiers met. This was on the 3rd June 1944 and lasted for a day or two. The august body had travelled from London to Droxford in a number of first class railway coaches. Wickham station was closer to the Overlord Southwick House HQ but Droxford afforded more shelter from any enemy aircraft that might overfly the area. Droxford villagers maintain that it was here, in the siding, that the decision was made to delay D-Day and thus the launching of Operation OVERLORD. This was not so, but makes an interesting story for visitors. The Americans (*bless their cotton socks*) suggested that a spur railway line be constructed from the existing Meon Valley Railway to an area adjacent to Southwick House - which would be 'real useful'. Putting aside consideration of

Droxford Station

And they marched the troops from South Parade Pier, Southsea... (Sadly, the hotel in the background has been replaced by a nightclub or something or other).
THE NEWS

...along these rickety platforms,...
THE NEWS

...all the way to the embarkation point, off Southsea beach.
THE NEWS

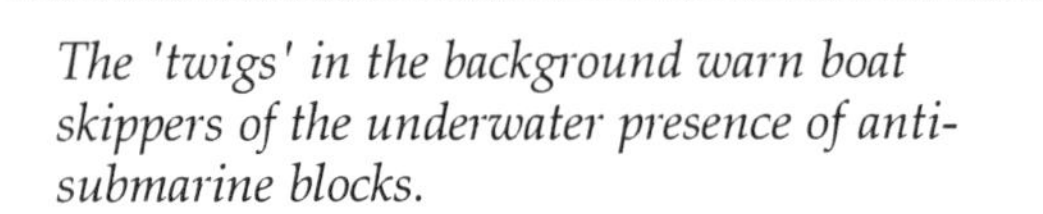

The 'twigs' in the background warn boat skippers of the underwater presence of anti-submarine blocks.

the extreme shortage of time available, coupled with the necessity to divert desperately needed men and materials from more pressing war work, the building of such a track would have been difficult to conceal from aerial reconnaissance. That would have resulted, inevitably, in unwelcome attention being drawn to Southwick House and its grounds. However, the proposal not being considered seriously, Droxford was used for the visit and achieved its niche in the history of the Second World War.*

**With Acknowledgements to 'The Meon Valley Railway' by R A Stone, published by Kingfisher Railway Productions.*

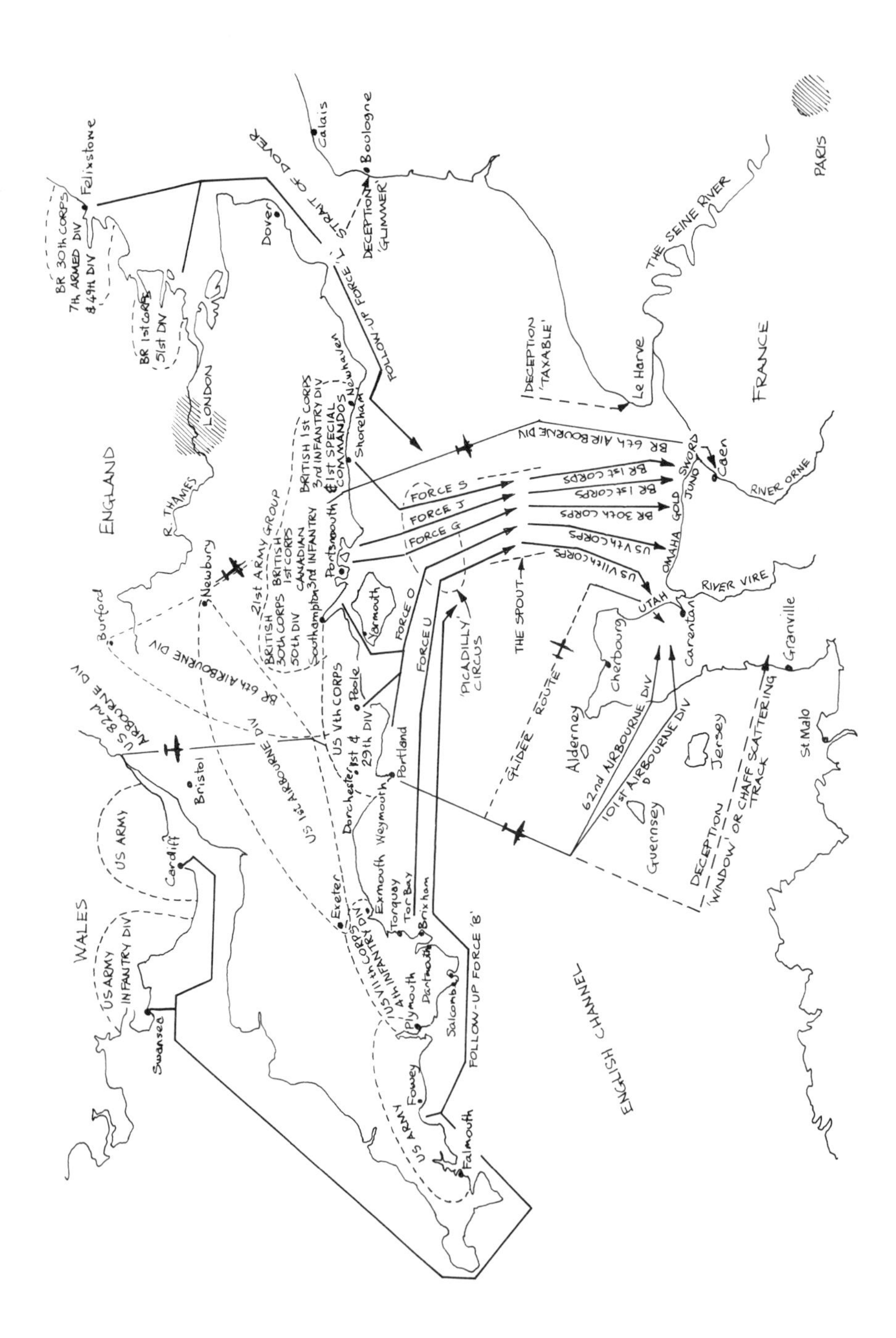

Illustration 12 D-Day Assault Plan detailing the Naval Operation NEPTUNE and Air Routes

This five franc note is a sample of the paper money issued to all the invasion troops as part of their 'standard' fighting kit.

This particular 'scrip' was one of a number showered down on Bertram and Violet Crook, Tom Bailey (who lived in the High St terrace and worked for the Crook family) and some of their children, amongst whom were Horace and Marjorie. It is to the latter that I am indebted for both the narrative and the loan of the currency.

As the tanks poured through Southwick Village, en route to their loading destinations, Bertram and his wife, who were landlord and landlady of the Red Lion Pub, passed up as many bottles of beer and packets of cigarettes as they could lay their hands on. The currency was gratefully given as a token of the troops' thanks. It could be no more, as it certainly wasn't legal tender in the UK.

Note the donor's signature. The notes were signed for, and on, when issued. I hope C. Smith had a 'good war'.

PRIVATE COLLECTION

Marjorie Coppin relates that the village did a roaring trade once the Mansion had been taken over, for not only were the two pubs popular haunts, but a NAAFI shop was set up in No. 56, one of the High St terrace of houses. This shop was in the care and control of a Lt Pugh.

A pair of giant sections, or Phoenix's, part of the Mulberry Harbours. These particular units were being assembled in Portsmouth Dockyard.

D-DAY MUSEUM

'Monty' on the bonnet of a jeep giving the lads a pep talk at a pre-invasion get-together.

THE NEWS

On the left is Lt Gen Miles Dempsey, Commander of the Second British Army, and, on the right, Maj Gen Percy Hobart. The latter officer, or boffin, was responsible for 'Hobart's Funnies', a collection of specially adapted armoured vehicles, mainly tanks, grouped together in the 79th Armoured Division. These 'funnies' were designed to flail a path through minefields, throw flames, lay bridges, carry ramps and launch giant mortar shells.

THE IWM

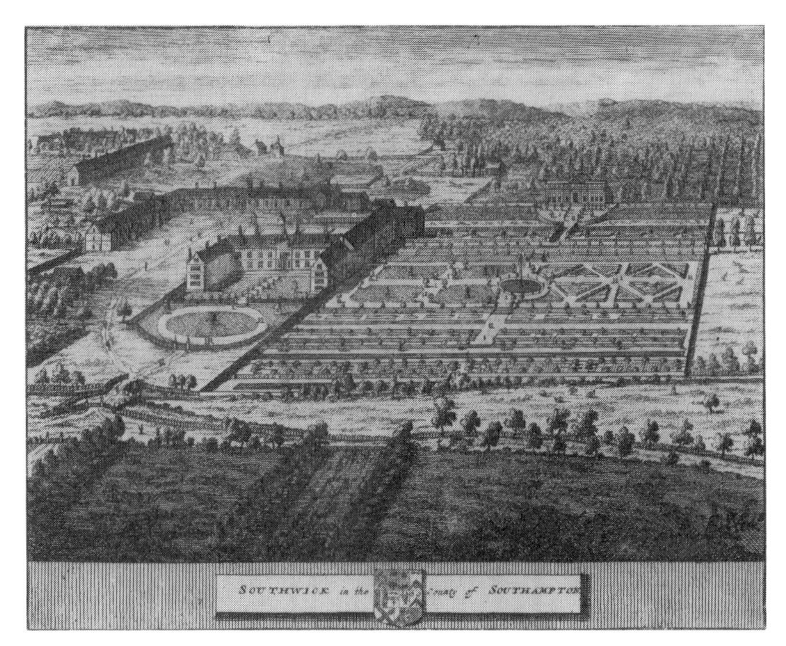

Kip's print of the original family Jacobean Mansion, circa 1732.

The ripples or 'slopes' were still in evidence prior to the construction of HMS Dryad's golf course.

PRIVATE COLLECTION

An 1820 Neale print of the two storey house that replaced the Jacobean Mansion.

PRIVATE COLLECTION

This Prosser print is a much lovelier piece of art than the rather primitive Neale effort (p.99). As does the Neale print, it represents the first of the two Thistlethwayte houses built on the same spot. The second, replacement building, with three storeys, and familiar to those who 'know and love' HMS Dryad, was constructed between 1840-1843, after the earlier one burnt down.

PRIVATE COLLECTION

This is Lee-on-Solent, where the tank crews are assembling to embark for the Channel crossing.
THE NEWS

Every soldier was issued with booklet 'French in one easy lesson'!
THE IWM

More armoured vehicles lining up for the 'off'.
THE NEWS

Brig Gen Elwood R. Quesada, Commanding Officer of the Ninth US Air Force Fighter Command (left), and Gen Eisenhower inspect fighter plane equipment whilst on a pre D-Day tour of inspection
The IWM EA18598

Brig A. Prain and Maj Gen J.D. Inglis share a conversation in the grounds of Southwick House.
The IWM H39172

Lt Col C. Norman outside the portals of The Mansion
The IWM H3174

This was the team organising the Southsea embarkation of troops.
THE NEWS

And the Royal Engineers mascot became part of the D-Day Invasion force. Perhaps he (or she) went for the ankles!

The News

These troops gather on the Southsea Esplanade for a group photograph. I'm not sure the angle of some of the headgear was at regulation tilt, especially the soldier kneeling on the right of the picture.

THE NEWS

How a sailor was included in the tank crew is a mystery. So was the obsession to take along a bicycle. Any number of pictures show them included as a mode of transport. In use they proved quite impractical.

THE NEWS

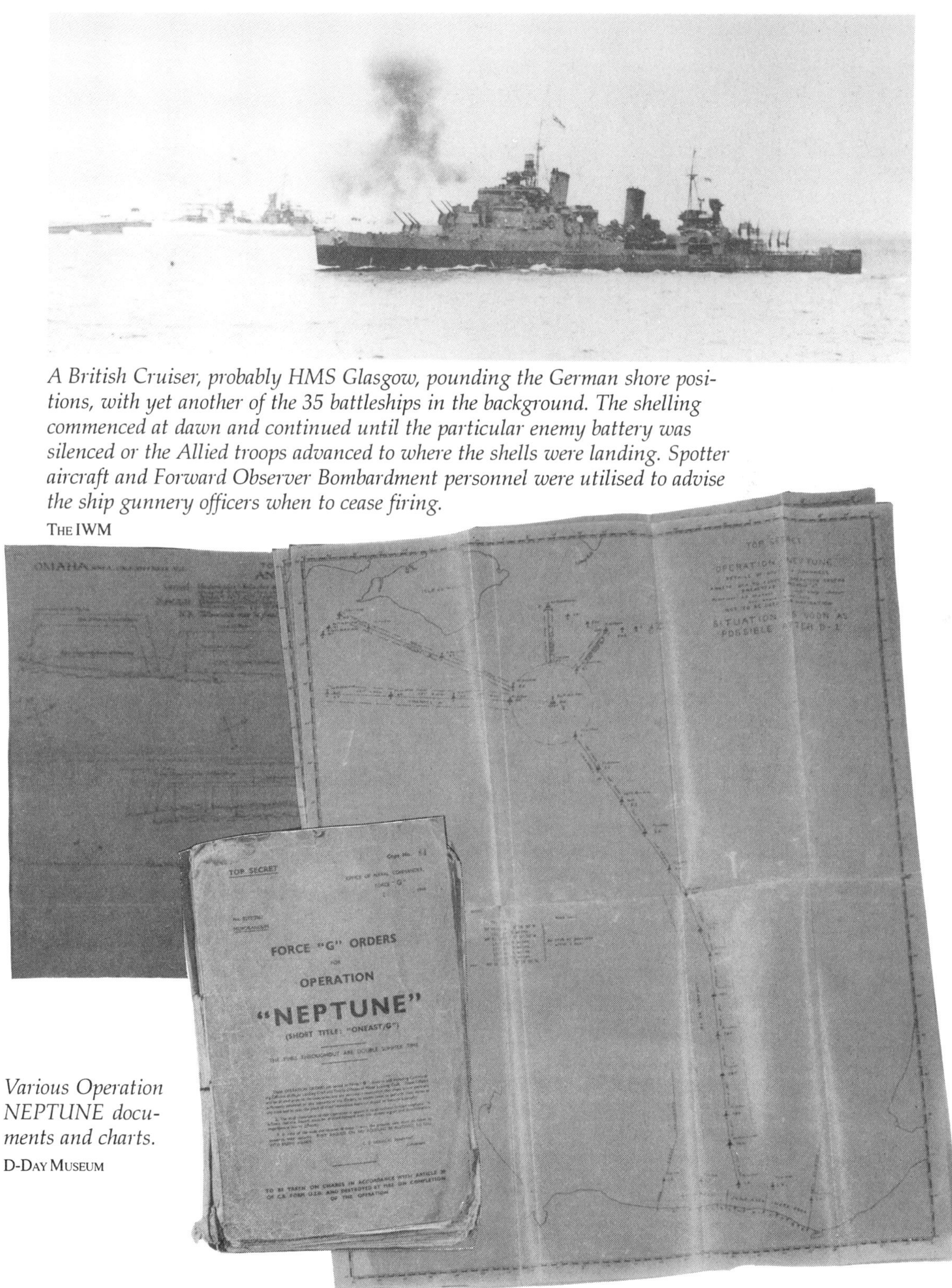

A British Cruiser, probably HMS Glasgow, pounding the German shore positions, with yet another of the 35 battleships in the background. The shelling commenced at dawn and continued until the particular enemy battery was silenced or the Allied troops advanced to where the shells were landing. Spotter aircraft and Forward Observer Bombardment personnel were utilised to advise the ship gunnery officers when to cease firing.
The IWM

Various Operation NEPTUNE documents and charts.
D-Day Museum

Maj Gen Richard Gale, commander of the British 6th Airborne Division, giving last minute words of encouragement to some of his men prior to boarding their plans. The Division was tasked with neutralising various objectives on the far eastern flank of the OVERLORD landings.
The IWM

To the right of the Major General's D-Day HQ is the 'Pegasus' pennant. This was to give its name to the Caen Canal or 'Pegasus' Bridge.
The IWM B5352

Those airborne troops that were conveyed by glider, took great risks. This Horsa glider, which carried some 20 men, as well as a jeep and trailer, suffered some damage on landing.
The American Airborne Divisions landing on the western flank of the invasion front incurred heavy losses, many due to their gliders breaking up on impact.
The IWM B5205

Due to lack of accurate information, the National newspapers had to make up much of the first day's news (what's new?). Some of the 'facts' were recycled German propaganda. For instance, the item in respect of 'Landings on Jersey, Guernsey' was totally inaccurate as the Channel Islands were left to their own devices for another year.

Still the Best! BIRD'S CUSTARD

Evening Standard

LONG JOHN

Churchill Announces Successful Massed Air Landings Behind Enemy in France

4000 SHIPS, THOUSANDS OF SMALLER VESSELS

"So Far All Goes to Plan"—11,000 First Line Airplanes

An immense armada of more than 4000 ships, with several thousand smaller craft, has crossed the Channel, said Mr. Churchill to-day, announcing the invasion.

"MASSED AIRBORNE LANDINGS HAVE BEEN SUCCESSFULLY EFFECTED BEHIND THE ENEMY'S LINES," HE SAID.

MR. CHURCHILL DESCRIBED THE LANDINGS AS THE "FIRST OF A SERIES IN FORCE ON THE EUROPEAN CONTINENT."

"The landings on the beaches are proceeding at various points at the present time. The fire of the shore batteries has been largely quelled, said Mr. Churchill.

"The obstacles which were constructed in the sea have not proved so difficult as was apprehended.

"The Anglo-American Allies are sustained by about 11,000 first line aircraft, which can be drawn upon as may be needed for the purposes of the battle.

No. 1

"Under the command of General Eisenhower, Allied naval forces, supported by strong air forces, began landing Allied armies this morning on the Northern coast of France."

SURPRISE

'LANDINGS ON JERSEY, GUERNSEY'

Thousands Of Fighters Strafe The Nazi Guns

SHELLED BY 640 GUNS

'Tanks Ashore on Normandy Coast'

—SAYS BERLIN

The Allies have established beach-heads in Northern France and are driving inland, according to pilots who have flown over the battle.

This afternoon the Germans announced that landings were continuing in the Seine Bay—the stretch of the Normandy coast between the two ports of Cherbourg and Le Havre.

The King on the Radio To-night

The 48th Marine Commandos pouring ashore, alongside men of the 8th Canadian Brigade, at St Aubin, on the Nan sector of JUNO Beach-head.

THE IWM B5218

I could not resist including these excellent photographs, although they are of European, post Breakout locations.

Gen Eisenhower visits 'Monty' at the latter's Normandy HQ...
THE IWM B9724

...and chats to a couple of Montgomery's Commanders.
THE IWM B5570

A year on, in March 1945, some of the outstanding British officers, under Gen Eisenhower's command, received American decorations, whilst similarly regarded Americans, under Montgomery's command, received British decorations. Left to right, seated, are (now) Field Marshal Montgomery, Gen Eisenhower and Gen Bradley. Standing, left to right, are Gen Creasey, Gen Simpson and Gen Dempsey.
THE IWM B14987

Chapter 6

The Village's D-Day 6th June 1944

It has been outlined how, due to various quirks of fate, Southwick Estate lost its treasured possession, the Mansion, the crown jewel as it were, to the Armed Forces. What could not have been realized, in those fraught and critical early days of the Second World War, was the dramatic and unique part the 'Big House' was to eventually play in the history of the War. How Southwick House was to become the very nerve centre for the D-Day landings, the building from whence the order was to be issued that would result in the Nazis being ousted from their illegal, repressive occupation of Western Europe, a bold and daring foray that was to end with the collapse of the Third Reich in the bomb torn bunkers of Berlin.

The Greatest Invasion Fleet Ever

The huge allied force, which sailed from the waters of the South Coast of England to liberate Europe, was the last and indeed the greatest of the many war fleets which, since Norman times, had sailed for France. The plan to assemble the fleet necessary to transport and protect the troops and machinery *en route* to the designated French beaches, pound the shore defences and secure the various bridgeheads were covered in the all embracing Operation NEPTUNE (Illus 11). This was the maritime arm of Operation OVERLORD and once these objectives were established, the plan dictated that the assault forces should fan out for the advance through northern Europe - last stop Berlin.

Operation NEPTUNE

On the 8th May Eisenhower and his air, land and naval Commanders (*See* Illus 10) agreed the tentative date for D-Day as the 5th June. (There are other May dates given for this first stab at the invasion day). Unfortunately, in the week before the appointed hour the weather started to deteriorate. The weather man chosen to head up a joint team of American and British experts and to act as Chief Meteorological Advisor to Eisenhower was one Group Capt J M

The Met Man

Manoeuvring about the mouth of Portsmouth Harbour.

THE NEWS

An Airborne wave of troops fly over the roofs of Portsmouth, en route to the Beach-heads.

THE NEWS

Clearing the channels, in this case off Hayling Island at the entrance to Langstone Harbour - 'Chimney conspic'!

THE IWM H35389

Stagg. He 'booked' into Southwick House at the end of May and from the 1st June there were twice daily meetings at which the details supplied were cogitated over. These 'get-togethers' were timed for 0400hrs and 2130hrs. The strain on General Eisenhower must have been tremendous, with advice and opinions coming at him from any number of directions. Not only had he to consider the views of his Deputy Commanders, but there were the British Prime Minister and American President's worries and political inputs which had to be taken into account. It was indeed a fortunate thing for the Allies that General Eisenhower, a relative 'unknown' until his appointment as the Supreme Commander, was such a calm, well balanced, uncomplicated, straightforward and thoughtful 'gentle man'. And even he was showing some signs of the pressure as the fateful day approached.

A Delay &...

On the 4th June, at 0430hrs, the planned date of the 5th was put back 24 hours due to a bad weather forecast which 'offered' high winds, low cloud and large seas. This baldly stated decision, to delay, nearly resulted in total disaster, as some craft were already under way! The necessity for the latter's early departure was due to the great distances which some of the assault forces had to travel. To arrive on station at the correct time, to steam south down the mine-swept channels of the The Spout (*See* Illus 12) and to 'hit' the specified beach at the designated H Hour, many vessels had to depart up to two days prior to D-Day. Flotillas of Force O, from Portland, and Force U, from Dartmouth, both loaded with American troops destined to land on UTAH and OMAHA Beach-heads, had 'set sail' on the 3rd June. Unfortunately, in the general state of confusion and appalling conditions, a convoy of some one hundred and thirty 128 LCT's (Landing Craft Tank) and their escort ploughed on - towards France. Oh dear! I imagine there was a fair amount of angst generated as the authorities set about trying to track down the missing convoy. Radio silence had to be maintained. The only courses of action open to the desperate men in charge were to throw up as many reconnaissance aircraft as there were to spare and to divert any fast warships that might be in the area. 'Don't panic'. In the event, the wayward flotilla were spotted by a Walrus flying boat, in failing light and lowering cloud cover, on the evening of the 4th. Closely following was a destroyer. The second attempt by the pilot to drop a message on to the lead ship succeeded and (it is reported), after an eternity, the convoy turned around. Phew!

Near Disaster

UTAH & OMAHA Beach-heads

The Midget Submarines

A lesser worry caused by the postponement was experienced by the crew of two midget submarines - X20 and X23. Their task was to each provide a lighted channel beacon for the early morning arrival of the massed assault craft as they closed on the French coast. They departed *HMS Dolphin*, Gosport, and cleared Portsmouth Harbour

The American landing craft gather...

THE IWM PL22379

...and GIs cluster to embark.

THE IWM PL22379

A dramatic shot of rows of Landing Craft anchored in the Solent 'awaiting the off'. The sea state is rather rough.

THE NEWS

entrance at 2215hrs on the night of the 2nd June. By the following day they were in their respective positions off the shore of Normandy. One was stationed at the west end of GOLD Beach-head, off Arromanches, and the other at the east end of SWORD Beach-head, off Ouistreham. Fortunately and without a hitch, they both received the signal heralding the temporary suspension of the invasion. On the other hand, the crew were forced to endure an extra 24 hours shut up within the tiny confines of their craft, submerged but riding out an extremely uncomfortable sea state, whilst bumping about on the sea-bed.

In addition to all the other predicaments thrown up by Operation OVERLORD, such as the vexed question of when to launch the invasion, there was one other 'weeny' fly in the ointment - a Gallic fly. The SHAEF staff were trying to persuade one General de Gaulle to co-operate. The single-minded, some would say obstructive, but without doubt, xenophobic leader of the Free French first collared Churchill, on the 4th June, in his train parked in the Droxford railway sidings. Later that day he travelled to Southwick House, where he harangued Eisenhower. It was deemed vital that De Gaulle encourage the French Resistance fighters to liaise and act in concert with the invasion troops. It may come as no surprise that in return the General was making widesweeping demands. Over the previous war years, a number of difficulties and sleights, real or imagined, had occurred between him and the Allied heads of government and military Commanders. As would any good strategist, the implacable De Gaulle seized his moment. He declared he would make the requisite broadcast - if the Allied governments recognized him as the sole ruler of France and that he alone should give orders to his fellow countrymen. These wishes were considered unreasonable and unacceptable, so the General refused to help during those vital few days. And we think we have problems with the French nowadays!

The Difficult General de Gaulle

...& Winston Churchill

Yet another difficulty for Eisenhower involved our very own Winston Churchill. He was insisting that he would accompany the invasion fleet on board a support ship, so as to be able to stand off the French coast during the first assault of the German held shores. Churchill was well known for his (no doubt well meaning) interference in Commanders' actions. Eisenhower, who had his hands pretty full at the time, refused Churchill permission on a number of grounds, not the least of which was the grand old man's personal safety. Churchill, not to be thwarted, advised the Supreme Commander that he (*Churchill*) could and would ship himself aboard one of His Majesty's ships, which were outside Eisenhower's immediate control. Fortunately for the supremo this particular dilemma was solved by some inspired, magisterial intervention and diplomacy. It came

The SHAEF team in conference at Southwick House early in June 1944. From left to right, seated are Air Chief Marshal Sir Arthur Tedder, Gen Eisenhower and Gen Sir Bernard Montgomery. Standing, left to right, are Lt Gen Omar Bradley, Admiral Sir Bertram Ramsey, Air Chief Marshal Sir Trafford Leigh-Mallory and Lt Gen Walter Bedell Smith.

THE IWM

The same officers but seated around a couple of deal, galley mess tables for a press conference.

THE IWM CH12109

about that King George VI heard of his Prime Minister's proposed 'jolly'. On so doing, he simply proclaimed that if Mr Churchill insisted on being present during the invasion, then, as King and titular head of the British Armed Forces, it would be his duty to lead his troops into action. Churchill quietly dropped his demand!

The King Intervenes

Any onlooker on the morning of 5th June, at 0330hrs, might well have observed General Eisenhower trudging a muddy mile to Southwick House, through 'a wind of hurricane proportions', with the rain absolutely sheeting down. It is reported that the wind was shaking and shuddering the temporary buildings and that the rain was beating a tattoo on the shuttered windows of the Mansion. In the old library were forgathered the various Commanders including Air Chief Marshall Tedder, Admiral Ramsay, Air Marshal Trafford Leigh-Mallory and General Montgomery. As if to convince the group of his infallibility, Group Capt Stagg confirmed that if the original date of the 5th had been proceeded with, the landings would probably have been severely disrupted, if not a complete disaster. On the other hand, despite the conditions prevailing as the meeting took place, the Chief Meteorologist opinioned that by the following day there was going to be some 36 hours of comparatively good weather. This would be accompanied by a reduced wind, calmer sea state and clearing clouds. But Eisenhower's decision was not that easy. What if the landings were to commence and then the weather unexpectedly closed in sooner than forecast, leaving the assault forces unsupported? (This was not to occur but it is a sobering thought that on the 19th June a violent storm broke and lasted for three days. During the course of that tempest the OMAHA Beach-head Mulberry Harbour was destroyed, and the one at the GOLD Beach-head was badly damaged. There's close!

The Met Man Divines...

Be that as it may, at 0415hrs General Dwight D Eisenhower made the historic announcement, variously reported as "Okay, we'll go" and "We will sail tomorrow". 'No one present disagreed'! D-Day was to be the next day, on the 6th June with H Hour (the time of the individual beach landings) between 0630hrs, on the UTAH Beach-head, and 0755hrs, on the SWORD Beach-head. The overall width of the invasion front was some 50 miles and the H Hour differences were due to the various equivalent times for similar heights of tide. The occasion is recorded by a plaque in the Map Room of *HMS Dryad* (Southwick House) celebrating the historic moment.

& Dwight says "Okay, we'll go"

IN THIS ROOM AT 04.15 ON THE
FIFTH DAY OF JUNE
NINETEEN HUNDRED AND FORTY-FOUR
GENERAL DWIGHT D EISENHOWER
THE SUPREME ALLIED COMMANDER

The UGHQ Plotting Room, Fort Southwick, tracking the D-Day invasion fleet.
The News

King George VI takes a great interest in progress.
The IWM HU16153

The Communications Room where all the incoming signals were decoded.
The IWM HU16151

MADE THE HISTORIC DECISION TO LAUNCH
THE ASSAULT AGAINST THE CONTINENT OF
EUROPE ON THE SIXTH DAY OF JUNE
DESPITE UNCERTAIN WEATHER CONDITIONS.
HAD THIS MAJOR DECISION
NOT BEEN MADE THE WHOLE OPERATION
WOULD HAVE HAD TO BE POSTPONED
UNTIL THE NEXT SUITABLE TIDAL PERIOD
A FORTNIGHT LATER.
ADVERSE WEATHER CONDITIONS
WHICH THEN AROSE MIGHT WELL HAVE
ALTERED THE WHOLE COURSE OF THE WAR

The Germans Get It Wrong

Strange to say, the foul weather that gave such concern to General Eisenhower and his staff, lulled the Germans into believing that any invasion would not take place, for at least 48 hours. Most Nazi Commanders went off to Paris for a conference (in respect of anti-invasion planning!) and Rommel travelled home to Germany to celebrate his wife's birthday.

The Wren's Tale Continues

The WRNS tale (cont):

> 'The weather at the beginning of June was very stormy. Dark skies, high winds and heavy rain - it was more like November.
> During this time, I was not allowed to go home. Every position on the switchboard had to be constantly manned, with internal calls heavily curtailed due to Overlord planning.
> Forty eight hours before the [*D-Day*] Landings there was a total silence on the switchboards, except for the Commander-in-Chief's personal line. Everyone was at their positions just waiting and waiting. With the terrible weather continuing, the atmosphere in UGHQ (Fort Southwick) was very tense.
> Early on the morning of the 6th June our waiting was ended. Officers of the three Services were standing around in groups and the strain showed on their faces. I had been on duty for 48 hours, with just short naps, and felt very tired.
> Suddenly, one of my young WRNS shouted, "Maam, Maam, something is coming through". The red light on the panel glowed brightly... I rushed to the position and listened. There it was - the long awaited code word which meant so much. They were through at last. A cheer went up and many young girls shed a tear. Maybe a boyfriend was over there - it was a very emotional moment - one which I shall never forget. I can still remember the thrill and relief of hearing the voices of our lads from that far Normandy shore. The terrible weather had led the Germans to believe we would not attack, but the crossing, already postponed from the 5th to the 6th June, could be delayed no longer. From Southwick House, General Eisenhower had made the decision that D-Day was to be 6th June, and I and my comrades at UGHQ were ready; waiting to receive word of those D-Day Landings'.

Despite Eisenhower's brave message, there were grave doubts concerning the success of the venture. These cannot better be illustrated than by noticing that the Supreme Commander had, on the 5th June, penned a 'fall-back' announcement along the following lines:

> '*Our landings in the Cherbourg-Le Havre area have failed to gain a satisfactory foothold and I have withdrawn the troops. My decision to attack at this time and place was based upon the best information available. The troops, the airforce and navy did all that bravery and devotion to duty could do. If any blame or fault attached to the attempt, it is mine alone.*'

Thank goodness these thoughts weren't leaked.

SUPREME HEADQUARTERS
ALLIED EXPEDITIONARY FORCE

Soldiers, Sailors and Airmen of the Allied Expeditionary Force!

You are about to embark upon the Great Crusade, toward which we have striven these many months. The eyes of the world are upon you. The hopes and prayers of liberty-loving people everywhere march with you. In company with our brave Allies and brothers-in-arms on other Fronts, you will bring about the destruction of the German war machine, the elimination of Nazi tyranny over the oppressed peoples of Europe, and security for ourselves in a free world.

Your task will not be an easy one. Your enemy is well trained, well equipped and battle-hardened. He will fight savagely.

But this is the year 1944! Much has happened since the Nazi triumphs of 1940-41. The United Nations have inflicted upon the Germans great defeats, in open battle, man-to-man. Our air offensive has seriously reduced their strength in the air and their capacity to wage war on the ground. Our Home Fronts have given us an overwhelming superiority in weapons and munitions of war, and placed at our disposal great reserves of trained fighting men. The tide has turned! The free men of the world are marching together to Victory!

I have full confidence in your courage, devotion to duty and skill in battle. We will accept nothing less than full Victory!

Good Luck! And let us all beseech the blessing of Almighty God upon this great and noble undertaking.

Dwight D. Eisenhower

D-DAY MUSEUM

21 ARMY GROUP

PERSONAL MESSAGE FROM THE C-in-C

To be read out to all Troops

1. The time has come to deal the enemy a terrific blow in Western Europe.

The blow will be struck by the combined sea, land and air forces of the Allies—together constituting one great Allied team, under the supreme command of General Eisenhower.

2. On the eve of this great adventure I send my best wishes to every soldier in the Allied team.

To us is given the honour of striking a blow for freedom which will live in history; and in the better days that lie ahead men will speak with pride of our doings. We have a great and a righteous cause.

Let us pray that "The Lord Mighty in Battle" will go forth with our armies, and that His special providence will aid us in the struggle.

3. I want every soldier to know that I have complete confidence in the successful outcome of the operations that we are now about to begin.

With stout hearts, and with enthusiasm for the contest, let us go forward to victory.

4. And, as we enter the battle, let us recall the words of a famous soldier spoken many years ago:—

"He either fears his fate too much,
Or his deserts are small,
Who dare not put it to the touch,
To win or lose it all."

5. Good luck to each one of you. And good hunting on the mainland of Europe.

B. L. Montgomery
General
C-in-C 21 Army Group.

1944

The Logistics & Statistics

The immensity of the scale of D-Day operations is difficult to imagine but the logistics and statistics include the following facts and figures:

> Of some some 1300 warships, 138 were major battleships, 221 were smaller combat vessels and 1000 were minesweepers and auxiliary craft. There were about 4000 landing craft, 800 merchant ships and 60 block ships, in addition to another 300 assorted boats. A total of 11,000 fighters, bombers, transports and gliders took part. Out of a total of approximately 2,500,000 men assembled, 250,000 were loaded in ships with 50,000 taking part in the initial frontal assault and 18,000 paratroops dropped into the battle zone. On the first day of the invasion troop losses by country amounted to: Americans 1,465; Canadian 335; and British circa 1,000.
> *To put these figures into some perspective, in 1916, on day one of the First World War Battle of the Somme about 20,000 British soldiers died. The period known as The Battle of the Somme lasted 19 weeks, between 4th July & 13th November during which 420,000 British, 200,000 French and 450,000 Germans died.)*
> By the evening of the 6th June 156,000 men had been landed. In the first three weeks of the D-Day, Lodgement and Breakout the total Allied death toll was 8,975.

Pour les encourages les autres both Eisenhower and Montgomery issued personal messages to be read out to the troops. That of the Supreme Commander General Eisenhower was heavy with compromise and gentle rejoinders not to 'rape, pillage or loot'! It read:

Eisenhower's Message

> 'You are soon to be engaged in a great undertaking - the invasion of Europe. Our purpose is to bring about, in company with our Allies and our comrades on other fronts, the total defeat of Germany. Only by such a complete victory can we free ourselves and our homelands from the fear and threat of the Nazi tyranny.
> A further element of our mission is the liberation of those people of Western Europe now suffering under German oppression.
> Before embarking on this operation, I have a personal message for you as to your own individual responsibility, in relation to the inhabitants of our Allied countries. As a representative of your country, you will be welcomed with deep gratitude by the liberated peoples, who for years have longed for this deliverance. It is of the utmost importance that this feeling of friendliness and goodwill be in no way impaired by careless or indifferent behaviour on your part. By a courteous and considerate demeanour, you can on the other hand do much to strengthen that feeling.
> The inhabitants of Nazi occupied Europe have suffered great privations and you will find that many of them lack even the barest necessities. You, on the other hand, have been and will continue to be provided adequate food, clothing and other necessities. You must not deplete the already meagre local stocks of food and other supplies by indiscriminate buying, thereby fostering the 'Black Market,' which can only increase the hardship of the inhabitants.
> The rights of individuals, as to their persons and property, must be scrupulously respected, as though in your own country. You must remember

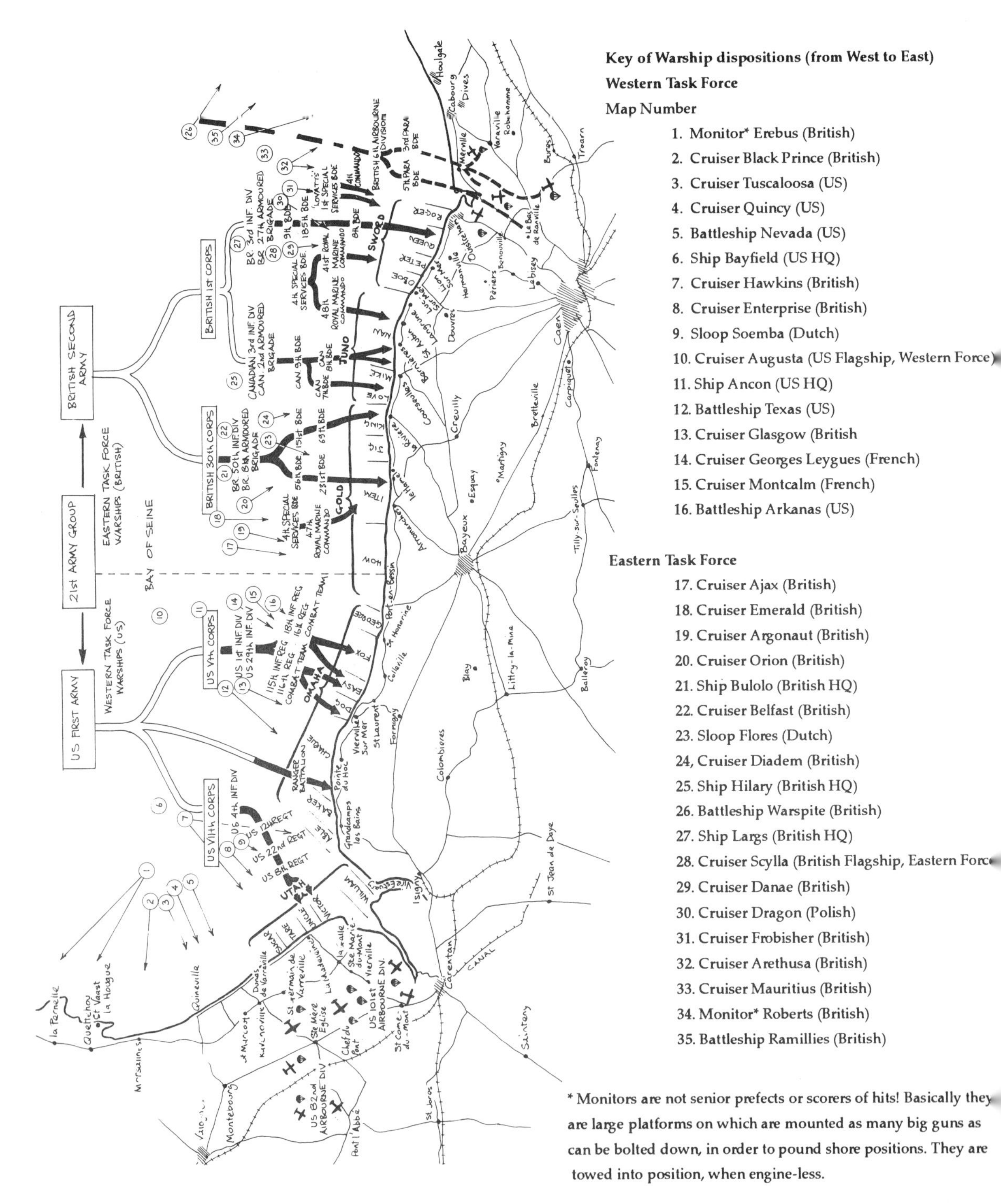

Illustration 13 D-Day Beach-head detail

always, that these people are our friends and Allies.
I urge each of you to bear constantly in mind that by your actions not only you as an individual, but your country as well, will be judged. By establishing a relationship with the liberated peoples, based on mutual understanding and respect, we shall enlist their wholehearted assistance in the defeat of our common enemy. Thus shall we lay the foundations for a lasting peace, without which our great effort will have been in vain.'

The *billet-doux* from General Bernard Montgomery was penned by a chap coming out of his corner fighting and was as follows:

Monty's Sermon

1. The time has come to deal the enemy a terrific blow in Western Europe.
   The blow will be struck by the combined sea, land and air forces of the Allies - together constituting one great Allied team, under the supreme command of General Eisenhower.
2. On the eve of this great adventure I send my best wishes to every soldier in the Allied team.
   To us is given the honour of striking a blow for freedom which will live in history and in the better days that lie ahead men will speak with pride of our doings. We have a great and righteous cause.
   Let us pray that 'The Lord Mighty in Battle' will go forth with our armies and that His special providence will aid us in the struggle.
3. I want every soldier to know that I have complete confidence in the successful outcome of the operations that we are now about to begin.
   With stout hearts and with enthusiasm for the contest, let us go forward to victory.
4. And, as we enter the battle, let us recall the words of a famous soldier spoken many years ago:
   'He either fears his fate too much,
   Or his deserts are small.
   Who dare not put it to the touch,
   To win or lose it all.'
5. Good luck to each one of you. And good hunting on the mainland of Europe.

Illustration 13 shows the D-Day Beach-head detail. From UTAH, to the west of the Bay of Seine, across to the eastern edge of SWORD, and beyond - an overall front of some 108,600yds, 61.7 miles or 98.9km. There's wide!

Admiral Ramsay was not to be left out of the 'battle of the messages'.

D-DAY MUSEUM

SPECIAL ORDER OF THE DAY
TO THE OFFICERS AND MEN OF THE
ALLIED NAVAL EXPEDITIONARY FORCE.

It is to be our privilege to take part in the greatest amphibious operation in history—a necessary preliminary to the opening of the Western Front in Europe which in conjunction with the great Russian advance, will crush the fighting power of Germany.

This is the opportunity which we have long awaited and which must be seized and pursued with relentless determination: the hopes and prayers of the free world and of the enslaved peoples of Europe will be with us and we cannot fail them.

Our task in conjunction with the Merchant Navies of the United Nations, and supported by the Allied Air Forces, is to carry the Allied Expeditionary Force to the Continent, to establish it there in a secure bridgehead and to build it up and maintain it at a rate which will outmatch that of the enemy.

Let no one underestimate the magnitude of this task.

The Germans are desperate and will resist fiercely until we out-manœuvre and out-fight them, which we can and we will do. To every one of you will be given the opportunity to show by his determination and resource that dauntless spirit of resolution which individually strengthens and inspires and which collectively is irresistible.

I count on every man to do his utmost to ensure the success of this great enterprise which is the climax of the European war.

Good luck to you all and God speed.

B. H. Ramsay

ADMIRAL.
ALLIED NAVAL COMMANDER-IN-CHIEF,
EXPEDITIONARY FORCE.

NAVAL COMMANDER
-3 JUN 1944

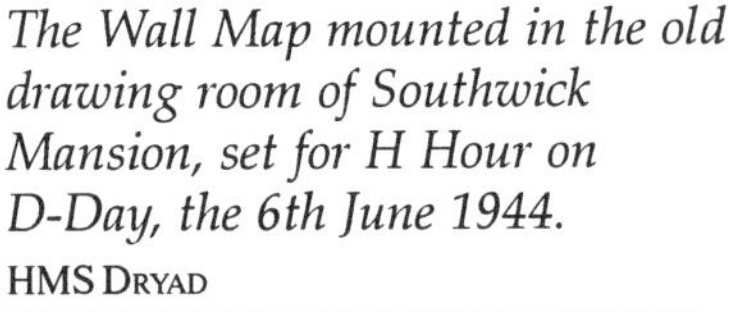

The Wall Map mounted in the old drawing room of Southwick Mansion, set for H Hour on D-Day, the 6th June 1944.

HMS DRYAD

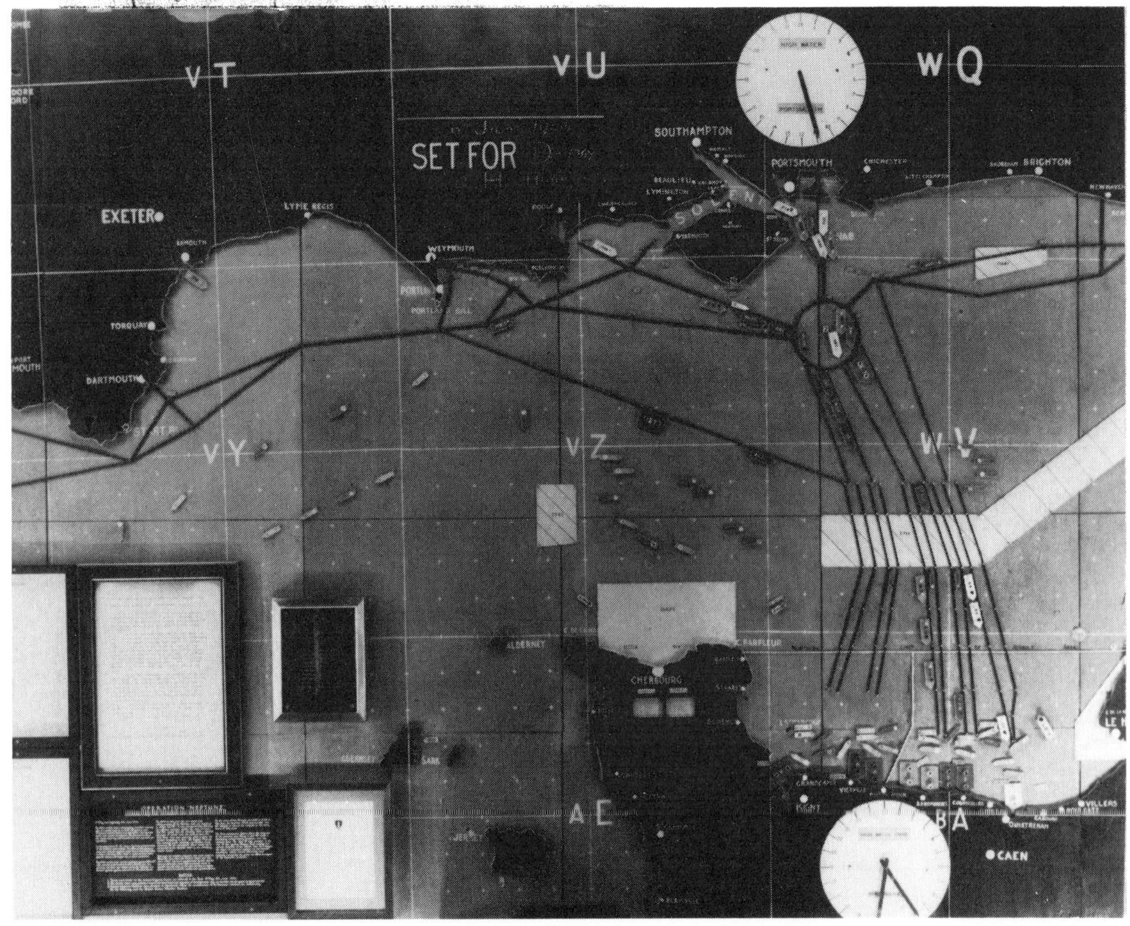

Chapter 7

The Village Fights On

1944 & On

The Map Clock Stops

Meanwhile, back at the ranch, or more exactly Southwick House, the main body of the headquarters remained in place. This state of affairs existed for some two weeks, but the D-Day map clock stopped at H Hour plus 34 hours.

The Commanders Depart &...

Naturally, the various Commanders and 'supporting cast' were in an absolute lather to touchdown on French soil and there was an almighty rush to get there. Montgomery embarked on a destroyer late on D-Day with the stated objective of finding a suitable location at which to establish his advance headquarters. Eisenhower boarded another destroyer, the next day, to visit OMAHA Beach-head and make a sea trip to the other invasion beaches. During the course of the latter, the Captain managed to run the ship aground at high speed. The damage sustained was so serious that Eisenhower and his entourage had to transfer to another vessel to return to England. Whoops! I would imagine there were some red faces on the bridge.

The Luminaries Arrive

Churchill finally made his way to France on D-Day plus 6 days to meet Montgomery. He is reputed to have sent President Roosevelt a note with the message 'Wish you were here'. Tactless! King George VI stepped ashore on the continent on D-Day plus 10.

Most commentators were to record, once the troops, machines and ships had left for France, that the lanes and roads, the copses, woods and fields, the villages, towns and cities, the ports and harbours and the waters of the Solent were all eerily quiet and deserted. The most tangible reminder of their presence were the chalked 'Thank You's'. These had been left behind by the crews of the vehicles which had been marshalled along the thoroughfares and were dedicated to the local populace who had helped make their enforced stopover the more bearable. These poignant messages were scrawled on the pavements, kerbstones and surface of the roads. On the other hand Southampton's docks remained incredibly busy, loading food, munitions, stores, vehicles and weapons to feed and supply the invasion forces. American personnel filled the vacant troop marshalling bases and camps as that City became their major port. In just

An evocative artist's view of the Wall Map Room during the build up to H Hour. Perhaps the somewhat leisurely, chatty ambiance is due to post-operational artistic licence?
HMS DRYAD

The Wall Map after restoration.
THE NEWS

four months the facilities handled outward cargo that equalled all the inward and outward shipments of the year before the war. I wonder just what went astray?

The Return Loads...

Mind you, it was only a matter of days before returning ships were to be disembarking human cargos of Allied casualties and German prisoners of war. For the initial weeks of the invasion bridgehead there simply wasn't enough available Normandy 'real estate' on which to create the 'Mash units' and POW camps. Once space allowed, these 'return loads' slowed to a trickle. Both Portsmouth and Southampton were well provided with hospitals - Haslar at the mouth of Portsmouth Harbour and the Royal Victoria Military at Netley, on the east shore of Southampton Water. Despite their convenient location, they were considered to be vulnerable to reprisal enemy bombing raids. It was thought these might be stepped up in a German effort to slow down the Allied advance. In addition, spies had advised of the planned rocket attacks. With these facts in mind, the plan was that Haslar and the Royal Victoria would be utilised as rapid transit bases for all but the most desperate cases. 'Holding' facilities were created at St James' Hospital, Portsmouth, The Royal Hopital, Mile End, and Queen Alexandra's, Cosham, in addition to sick bays at a number of the Naval bases spaced about Portsmouth Harbour. All other casualties were to be transported further inland to the large County facilities. Captured Axis troops were landed at Portsmouth, Gosport and Southampton. Those captives who were wounded were transported to a primitive POW camp of Nissen huts inside the grounds of Queen Alexandra's Hospital. The healthy POW's were disembarked at the Hardway, just to the north of Gosport (from whence, only days before, had cast-off landing craft laden down with Allied troops, tanks and trucks). From Hardway the prisoners were marched along the narrow, pinched streets, lined with terraced houses, to nearby Forton Barracks. Axis prisoners shipped to Southampton were placed in camps that had sprung up beside Western Esplanade and the dock areas. Southwick played its part, hosting these 'guests' at the Creech Woods Army base. Of the latter, only some footings, mostly concealed by undergrowth and trees, remain as mute testament to the woodlands' wartime effort.

The Wounded

& Prisoners

The Map Room Is Abandoned

In the hurly-burly of the post-invasion, the Southwick House Map and Map Room were simply abandoned. It was not until well after the return of the Navigation School that the historic importance of the various artifacts was appreciated. They were restored and the Map was repositioned to detail the locations of the various forces at H Hour on D-Day. At the official unveiling, on the 7th August 1946, Rear Admiral Creasy, who had been Admiral Ramsay's Chief of Staff during Operation OVERLORD, was to say " ...this

The Invasion force may have landed and established a beach-head, but they required massive, continuing support in the shape of men, machines and supplies. In the month of July 1944, at Lee on Solent, a mobile crane is being taken on board,...
(The censor has 'whited' out the IOW).
THE NEWS

...a landing craft powers its way out of Portsmouth Harbour for French shores...
THE NEWS

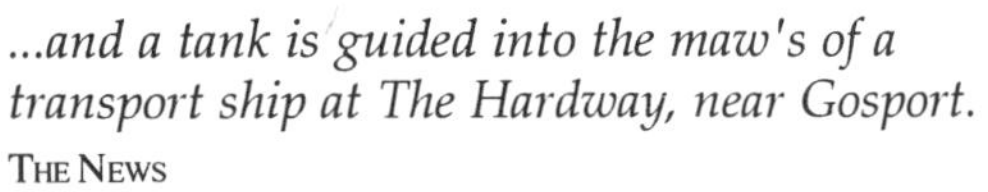

...and a tank is guided into the maw's of a transport ship at The Hardway, near Gosport.
THE NEWS

Moreover, our coastline continued to need cover. This is a snapshot of the Southsea Common battery 'welcoming' intruders.
THE NEWS

house was in fact the literal pin-point of the invasion operation ..."*.

A touching tale involved an ex 'Wren' who had been on duty in the Map Room during the fateful period of D-Day. On a 'guided' tour, many years later, she shed a tear as one of her tasks had been to move the counters representing the movement of the various craft. At the time she had been convinced she was sending men to their death.**

Admiral Ramsey's Sad Demise

The first floor of Southwick House was still in its pre-war, original state of separation, harking back to the days when master and servant were sealed off from each other. It was opened up in October 1944 after the final departure of the Invasion HQ, Admiral Sir Bertram Ramsay having left on 8th September. It is very sad to relate that this remarkable officer, who had masterminded the Naval operations of both Dunkirk in 1940 and D-Day in 1944, was not to reap the peacetime benefits and plaudits of his almost superhuman efforts. He was to die in an air crash in 1945.

With acknowledgements to 'Navigation and Direction The Story of HMS Dryad' by Vice Admiral B B Schofield, published by Kenneth Mason, Emsworth.

***For this snippet, I am indebted to a letter from Len Bridge, National Secretary of the Coastal Forces Veterans Association.*

An illustration of a commemorative tray hanging in the Wardroom of HMS Dryad...

... and a detail.

HMS DRYAD

CHAPTER 8

EPILOGUE

The Navigator's Return

The departure of the 'invasion team' from Southwick House presented the returning Navigators (from Greenwich) with a mixed bag of 'left-overs'. Their's was the fortune to find themselves the proud possessors of about 100 Nissen huts, in addition to jumble of other abandoned miscellanea.

Various tactical training buildings, simulators and models, whose completion had been held up by Operation OVERLORD, were completed during the next few years. It was a 'crying shame' that the Navigation School had proved so successful and that it was not able to squeeze back into its former premises at Portsmouth Dockyard.

Mr Borthwick Inherits

In 1944 Hugh Frank Pakenham Borthwick-Norton became the new owner of Southwick Estate. At the time of succeeding to the inheritance he had been plain Mr Borthwick. To renew links with his very famous Southwick forebears, he added the surname suffix Norton to his own. He inherited the holdings from his rather distant relation Colonel Evelyn Thistlethwayte. Almost immediately he instigated enquiries regarding the restoration of Southwick House and its grounds to the Estate. In the normally tardy way of anybody not wishing to own up, the Navy took until 1948 to admit that it was going to compulsorily purchase the Mansion and Park. Negotiations commenced. There is no doubt that the new Lord of the Manor devoutly wished the property to be returned and it was only a few months after the eventual purchase of Southwick House and the 295 acre Park that Mr Borthwick-Norton died. The price paid of £40,000 on the 7th July 1950 was absolutely ludicrous, but I am sure it was the dashed hopes of the return of the Estates' focal point, not the money involved, that proved so heartbreaking. It was a pity that the words of the First Sea Lord at war's end were not heeded. He complained bitterly that the navigators should go back to the vicinity of the sea.

The Requisitioning of Southwick House...

& Renaming

In 1950 a visiting officer opinioned that *HMS Dryad*, as it was now named, was little more than a motley collection of buildings, incorporating the old house, stables, the farm and row upon row of mangy Nissen huts. Naturally enough, implementation of the proposed plans for the development of the site were delayed until the final outcome of the compulsory purchase were completed. Once finalized, various long-overdue changes took place immediately,

This post war aerial view of Southwick House reveals that Boulter Lane has not yet been lined with housing. A splendid avenue of trees still marks the sunken holloway of the old driveway.
HMS DRYAD

In this later shot much of the tree cover (which made the Mansion such an ideal location (or the OVERLORD HQ) has been removed.
HMS DRYAD

including knocking down most of the trees around the house - referred to as a 'notable deforestation'. Towards the end of the decade more construction threw up even more ancillary buildings.

General Eisenhower Revisits

On the 6th August 1963, General Eisenhower, who had in the meantime been elected and served his term of office as President of the United States of America, returned to *HMS Dryad* to take a nostalgic look over the scene of his dramatic decision.

Continued Improvements

About 1964 a five-year plan was drawn up on which work started in earnest. In 1965 a painting of the Normandy Invasion by Norman Wilkinson, completed from sketches made on the bridge of *HMS Jervis* at the time of the D-Day landings, was unveiled by Vice-Admiral Sir John Frewen. A new administration and instruction building (of particularly unpleasant external appearance) was completed in 1966 and named Oliver Block in memory of the 'founding Admiral' of the Navigation School. Cunningham Block, noticeable for its thermal cladding, and housing state-of-the-art computer equipment for training purposes, was constructed in 1968. The modernization of Southwick House took place in 1970 and resulted in '...the old house being improved out of all recognition'. Yes, I'm sure it was! WRNS' quarters were constructed and in July 1973 the Establishment received the supreme accolade of a visit from Her Majesty, Queen Elizabeth II, and husband Prince Philip. As their cavalcade of cars swept through the village he was reported to have pointed out the Golden Lion (the lounge bar of which had been the officers' unofficial mess during the War years).

The Queen & Prince Philip Drop In

The association of the old Southwick Mansion with the Nation's warfare was to continue, as dramatically re-emphasised in 1982. In that year, Britain, in probably its last colonial extravaganza, decided to retake the Falklands islands. It was at *HMS Dryad* that the simulated war scenarios were planned and fought out, thus enabling our warship Captains to have the benefit of pre-conflict scheming and training. So, little in history is new, as graphically illustrated by the continuing tradition of tiny Southwick Village being the operations centre of military conflict with the 'known' world, a tradition lasting some 650 years, starting with Edward III in 1338 and still maintained in the 1980s.

Secretive, Southwick may have been, but certainly never uninteresting and, to significantly misquote a certain Doctor:

> *He who is tired of Southwick, he is tired of life for there is in Southwick all that history can afford.*

As a postcript, 'my hero' General Montgomery, who probably ranked as the greatest British General since Wellington, told his men on the eve of D-Day:

Southwick House not many years after the end of the war...

...and in the late 1960s.

HMS DRYAD

> 'To us is given the honour to strike a blow for freedom which will live in history and in the better days that lie ahead, men will speak with pride of our doings.'

He was never defeated in battle, yet had organised a war machine of far greater size than any commanded by his predecessors in British History. He died at Alton, Hampshire in March 1978.

GLOSSARY

The lead-up to and finalisation of Operation OVERLORD (the plan and operation to invade France in the Spring of 1944) inevitably caused a fine 'crop' of Code Names.
ANVIL Planned Allied landings on the coast of the South of France, scheduled for August 1944. Renamed DRAGOON.
BODYGUARD Overall 'plan of deceipt' to mislead the Axis command, covering the overall Allied strategy in Europe. *See* FORTITUDE.
BOLERO The build-up of US men, machines and supplies, in the UK, necessary for OVERLORD.
BOMBARDON Breakwaters tied into the MULBERRY Harbours.
CORNCOB Blockships forming part of GOOSEBERRY.
CROSSBOW Allied air attacks to eliminate the threat of the V-1 and V-2 weapons.
FORTITUDE Plan to cover a feint in the direction of the Pas de Calais area, to draw attention away from the true thrust of OVERLORD.
GOLD This (British) beach-head was bounded by Port-en-Bessin to the west and La Riviere in the east, with the sectors of How, Item, Jig and King.
GOOSEBERRY An artificial breakwater associated with the MULBERRY Harbours and other offshore anchorages.
JUNO The smallest (Canadian) beach-head which almost reached the village of La Riviere to the west, where the front was bounded by the GOLD beach-head, and the village of Luc-sur-Mer to the east, where SWORD beach-head took over. From west to east, the sectors that made up JUNO were, Love, Mike and Nan.
MAPLE The mine-laying activities associated with Operation NEPTUNE.
MULBERRY Artificial harbours to facilitate the OVERLORD shipping requirements.
NEPTUNE The naval operations in respect of OVERLORD.
OMAHA The easterly one of the two American beach-heads and the largest of the five invasion fronts. From the west, where it butted up to UTAH, in the Vire Estuary, it ran almost all the way to the town of Port-en-Bessin. Its sectors were the most recallable and evocative, being Charlie, Dog, Easy, Fox and George.
PHOENIX Concrete caissons and barges, part of the MULBERRY Harbour project.
PLUTO Pipe Line Under The Ocean - to supply fuel requirements associated with Operation OVERLORD from the south of England to the French coast.
POINTBLANK Allied bomber offensive.
RANKIN A, B & C. Alternative plans in the event of German weakening or surrender, prior to Overlord.
REDBALL One-way express routing for vehicles at the various beach-heads.
ROUNDUP Operation planned for a 1943 invation of France in the Pas de Calais area.
SLEDGE HAMMER - An aborted, if limited, continental bridgehead planned for 1942 at Cherbourg to divert Axis troops from the Eastern Front. Superseded by ROUNDUP.
SWORD This (British) beach-head marked the eastern end of the overall invasion front. It stretched almost to the village of Langrune in the west, where it adjoined JUNO, to Ouistreham in the east, where the beach-head BAND would have taken over, if it had been activated. Its sectors were Oboe, Peter, Queen and Roger. Admittedly the Parachute Brigades 'dropped in' along a corridor at the east end of the SWORD beach-head.
TOMBOLA Fuel piped from tankers to storage tanks on the French soil.
UTAH The (American) bridge-head originally bounded by the Dunes of Varreville, in the north-west, to the Estuary of the River Vire, in the south-east. The original sectors that made up this bridge-head were (from top to bottom) Queen, Roger, Sugar, Tare, Uncle, Victor and William.
Only Uncle and Victor were finally targetted..
WHALE Pierheads bridging the gap between the MULBERRY Harbours and the shore.
WILDFLOWER Gt Britain

Printed by The Lavenham Press Ltd., Lavenham, Suffolk, England.